CRITERIA
FOR PLANNING
THE COLLEGE AND UNIVERSITY
LEARNING RESOURCES CENTER

Irving R. Merrill
Harold A. Drob

Published by

Association for Educational
Communications and Technology
1126 16th St., N.W.
Washington, D. C. 20036

Library of Congress Cataloging in Publication Data

Merrill, Irving Rodgers, 1919-
  Criteria for planning the college and university
learning resources center.

  Edition for 1974 published under title:
Criteria for planning the university learning
resources center.
    Includes bibliographical references.
    1. Libraries, University and college--Administration.
2. Instructional materials centers--Administration.   I. Drob,
Harold A., joint author.
II. Title.
Z675.U5M43   1977   027.7   77-2612
ISBN 0-89240-003-X

AECT President: Richard Gilkey
AECT Executive Director: Howard Hitchens
Editor: Clint Wallington
Design and Production: Sandy Spicer

Stock No. 035

Additional copies of this book may be purchased by writing to
the Publications Department, Association for Educational
Communications and Technology, 1126 16th St., N.W., Washington, D.C. 20036.

Foreword

The original study on which this book is based was initiated in 1969 at the request of the University of California's President's Advisory Committee on Learning Resources on behalf of the University of California community, which included faculty, students, learning resources center directors, administrators, and planning and budgeting officers. The purpose of the first study was to identify the essential criteria for planning university learning resources centers. The term learning resource center means an *active program* for the development, utilization and evaluation of learning resources in the instructional process.

The original study was first proposed by R.V. Walen, University Educational Facilities Planner in the Office of the President. The criteria on staff and space were developed with the assistance of Thomas L. Banks, Wayne Emery, Ray A. Litke, and John W. Thorne of the Communications Office for Research and Teaching, University of California at San Francisco. Barry H. Clagett of the University's Budget Office offered many constructive comments on planning the budget, as did Mr. Walen. The study report has benefited from the review of successive drafts by senior persons responsible for learning resources on each UC campus, including Kent W. Bishop, Bernard N. Desenberg, Phillip E. Frandson, Gary N. Hess, Thomas J. Karwin, Peter C. Kerner, Charles L. Nearing, Joseph J. Sayovitz, and Robert D. Tschirgi.

The material in the study, with some modification, forms the basis for this book. Chapter 1 presents a general definition of learning resources that applies to conventional as well as innovative forms of instruction along with background information relating to the growth and effectiveness of learning resources and some present misconceptions about them. Chapter 2 traces briefly the historical trend especially within the University of California system toward the establishment of campuswide centers for learning resources in order to achieve greater savings, improved instructional effectiveness, and an additional contribution to institutional coherence. Chapter 3 indicates that these advantages will be achieved only if valid administrative criteria for management, decentralization, and controls and standards are adopted. Chapter 4 presents current criteria for numbers of staff and square feet of space within a university learning resources center. Chapter 5 describes how the recommended planning-programming-budgeting system can be applied to the learning resources center budget and takes up several critical budgetary considerations affecting learning resources management.

Criteria are stated in this study if the weight of evidence clearly supports them. Problems needing further examination are reported if they are urgently needed for planning but evidence is ambiguous or insufficient. The few areas in which evidence is lacking are identified if it is likely that they may become important in the future.

The evidence consists of several types of data. To begin with, available studies, experiments, surveys, and other research on learning resources in a university setting were examined. These data were then compared with the results of a mail survey conducted by the authors on current practices at the University of California. The findings of this nine-campus survey were cross-checked by personal interviews. In addition, a small research project was conducted by the authors to develop hitherto unavailable criteria for staff and space. We thank all those who made this possible and welcome the comments of our colleagues.

Irving R. Merrill
Harold A. Drob

Preface

AECT has been, and still is, acutely aware of the guidelines for developing learning resources programs for colleges and universities. The nature and diversity of these institutions—as contrasted with elementary and secondary schools—make the establishment of a single set of standards quite difficult. One institution may rely heavily on television in an educational outreach program. A small campus may concentrate on an auto-tutorial approach with materials at the learning resources center. Some institutions stress technical areas and lean toward specialized cooperative programs.

The authors, Irving Merrill and Harold Drob, have taken a major step in finding—and testing—some common elements for all programs—particularly space and staff. Their planning criteria for areas and personnel range from the usual audiovisual services to instructional development. Further, Merrill and Drob have presented criteria for levels of service within these areas and a range of campus sizes. Most important, they have linked these to the common denominator, student learning.

AECT has recently adapted a policy to insure that the terminology used in its monographs conforms to that in its published definition and terminology glossary. This publication was in press before the aforementioned policy went into effect and some of the terminology used by the authors may differ from generally accepted AECT usage. Please keep this in mind as you read the book.

The criteria presented by Merrill and Drob, developed through research in the University of California system, are equally applicable to colleges and universities across the country. AECT is proud to bring them to you and we hope you will find them useful. As always, we welcome your comments in our continuing dialogue.

Clint Wallington

Table of Contents

Learning Resources: Growth, Effectiveness, Present Misconceptions

Learning resources have been associated with higher education since the days of antiquity. While books have been the more traditional medium, other learning resources have been used. Aristotle used the *camera obscura* as a teaching device for his students at the Lyceum in 330 B.C. Anatomical drawings of high scientific accuracy were used at the University of Padua as early as 1543 A.D. The magic lantern, an early type of slide projector, was invented in Germany in 1870 and was in use in German universities only a few years later. Research had been completed demonstrating the educational value of motion pictures as early as 1917, following Edison's demonstration of a prototype in 1894. No one aware of these facts can deny that learning resources, print and nonprint, judiciously used, have played an important role in improving the effectiveness of the traditional approach to instruction.

The traditional approach is still the most widely accepted in higher education; it involves small classes, discussion-type interaction, and teaching in a personalistic fashion [Dubin and Taveggia, 1968]. The use of learning resources to support this approach has existed for so long, and has increased so gradually, that the practice has been virtually unrecognized. At a time when masters' theses and doctoral dissertations have probed every part of campus life, no academic study of the growth and development of learning resources, especially audiovisual materials, on any campus of the University of California has come to our attention—yet the value of portable media equipment (projectors, cameras, tape recorders) in active use on one of the smaller of the nine campuses alone came to more than $500,000 in 1968-69.

Since World War II new learning resources for higher education have appeared. The first was closed-circuit television, which has gained the broadest national acceptance. Following closely came the language laboratories, programmed learning, self-instructional laboratories, and computer-assisted instruction. These new media, it is generally agreed, are different. Discussion about them during the past 10 years has centered on the nature of this difference. Much of this difference is one of degree only, not of kind. To be sure, the systems are larger and more complex; they may require more technicians for operation; and they generally have the capability of serving more people for longer periods more efficiently.

A development of more fundamental significance since World War II is the emergence of new methods of teaching. Several of these methods challenge the assumed effectiveness of the traditional approach. In the absence of conclusive evidence, a lively intellectual crossfire among the several proponents has resulted. The scope of the present study does not permit a full description of each of these methods but they will be mentioned as necessary, because each of them provides for the use of new media. Although several of these methods are more than a decade old, widespread interest is recent and the ideas are still largely untried in most institutions of higher education [Brown and Norberg, 1965, p. 307]. But the conflict is primarily over approaches to teaching; new learning resources will be employed no matter which approach gains acceptance, because all of them, including the traditional approach, involve use of learning resources. Demand for learning resources in higher education is thus not likely to fall below its present level during the next two decades and will probably continue to increase.

As the need for additional learning resources, especially non-print materials, has developed, various names have been applied to the field. In 1923, the National Education Association established a Division of Visual Instruction designed to explore the effective use of lantern slides, filmstrips, and silent motion pictures. This organization changed to the Department of Audio-Visual Instruction in 1947, to include such new media as sound motion pictures, audiotape recorders, and sound recordings to accompany filmstrips. In 1970 the NEA formed a new Division of Educational Technology and the membership of the Department of Audio-Visual Instruction became a separate professional association called the Association for Educational Communications and Technology.

The use of a variety of terms, such as instructional media, instructional materials, learning centers, auto-tutorial instruction, and instructional technology reflects the vigorous growth of these resources and the healthy attention devoted to their function in higher education. In this book the term *learning resources* refers to this general field. We define learning resources centers to include the facilities for the origination, distribution, and display of audio, television, and graphic materials for group and individual presentation; the instructional materials thus created and recorded; and the persons employed to participate with the teacher in their creation, presentation, and evaluation.

For the purposes of this planning guide, this definition excludes most scholarly articles and books used for research instead of instruction. Programed texts and shorter written materials that are included as part of a carefully planned unit of instruction do fall within our definition of learning resources. The relation between the library and the learning resources center will be considered in Chapters 2 and 3.

A variety of classification schemes has been applied to learning resources over the past 20 years. The traditional approach viewed learning resources as material things that provide the vehicles for the auditory or visual messages, such as the chalkboard; the model; slide, opaque, and motion-picture projectors; and television. One extension of this approach is to classify learning resources as instructional media or instructional aids.

The *media* are said to constitute complete systems, such as television, that can carry the entire instructional message; whereas the *aids*, such as charts and slides, serve only to support a classroom teacher's face-to-face presentation [Bretz, 1969].

Another classification derives from computer technology. Equipment salesmen may refer to a rear projection motion picture playback unit as "hardware" and the cartridge, loaded with a continuous loop of 8mm film having a magnetic audio stripe, as the "software." The field of engineering lends the term "systems approach," involving the analysis of learning resources, the teacher, and the student as components of a "man-machine system" [Lee, 1970].

Currently, serious attention is given to a classification scheme derived from a psychological analysis of the conditions of learning. The role of the teacher is to manage the learning of the student so that at the completion of the unit of instruction the student is able to perform new skills. Specific behavioral objectives are stated, and the steps necessary to arrive at terminal behaviors from certain entry behaviors are analyzed. The decision as to how the media can make learning more efficient is repeated for each step of the analysis. Considered in this way, one is likely to classify learning resources according to the type of channel they offer, as follows: actual objects and events, representational pictures (static and moving), diagrammatic pictures, printed language, and auditory language [Gagne, 1970]. This variety of classification schemes is another indication of the importance of learning resources in higher education.

This chapter makes three main points, as follows:

There is a *requirements-pull* (on the part of faculty, students, and administrators) and a *technology-push* toward the growth of learning resources in higher education.

There is solid empirical evidence of the effectiveness of learning resources in higher education.

Three misconceptions have slowed, but not halted, the adoption of learning resources.

Considered together, these points indicate that learning resources will continue to increase in higher education.

The remainder of this chapter presents background information relating to the growth, effectiveness, and present misconceptions concerning learning resources—information needed before a reasonable plan for effective resources management can be developed.

GROWTH

Faculty Interest

Teaching styles vary with the individual teacher and with the type of subject matter to be covered. A mathematician may be able to teach effectively with only a chalkboard, but a physicist may require television, a turntable stage, motion pictures, and photographic slides. Another physicist may use only a chalkboard. These variations in style among good teachers must be respected because they help preserve the personal element that enriches learning. On the average, however, the past decade has seen increased use of learning resources by all teachers in higher education.

At least two factors have contributed to this growth. Use of films, charts, and models in the traditional approach to instruction has grown, a factor that may well be associated with the general increase in the faculty-student ratio. The new media are the other significant factor, a finding that is supported by two nationwide studies sponsored by the National Education Association. Thornton and Brown (1968) summarize their 1963 and 1967 studies of the new media in higher education as follows:

> In a period of only four years . . . there is undeniable expansion in the thoughtful application of previously reported new media to instruction. No innovative practice of promise at that time is now reported to have been abandoned for reasons of cost or faculty inertia; rather there is evidence of careful evaluation of results of experimental instruction and rapid development of more sophisticated and effective applications of practices that were at first adopted tentatively and unpretentiously.

Student Interest

In the early 1960s, as faculty members were beginning to use the new media in higher education, students occasionally expressed the fear that learning resources would be substituted for the teacher, producing a rigid factory-like curriculum. In the 1970s students tend to reject this assumption. Recently, in his "President's Column" in a University of California student newspaper, a student officer mentioning programed instruction and other modern educational methodology strongly agreed that they could be used to reduce the class hours in his curriculum. Making a precise discrimination between use of learning resources, of which he approves, and a presumed educational goal which he questions, he wrote:

> So the question—as it now stands—is should this campus react to this trend and reduce the total time allowed for graduation or use new educational methodology to reduce the class hours while keeping the same four year graduation schedule. (Hubiak, 1970, p. 3)

The first "TV generation" of students has now reached college and graduate school. Throughout their elementary and secondary education they have been taught by television, language laboratories, and programmed instruction. They have adopted as their own such devices as cassette tape recorders, earphones and headsets, and transistor radios. They know from personal experience the value of learning resources in reaching instructional objectives. The majority of this generation has come to expect their use in higher education.

Administrator Interest

If unlimited funds were available, planners and administrators could be expected to respond favorably to requests from faculty and students for increased use of learning resources. However, funds for higher education are severely limited during the 1970s. The problem that administrators must face is how to minimize costs while maintaining the quality of instruction. Their course of action must be based upon three available options: dilute, delete, and/or develop.

The first option to dilute instruction, as Dubin and Taveggia (1968) point out in their stimulating monograph, *The Teaching-Learning Paradox,* has already been exercised across the nation in two ways during the 1950s and 1960s. One, a *sub rosa* way, has been to use low-cost graduate teaching assistants in undergraduate instruction. The other, a more visible way of lowering instructional costs per student, has been to increase the size of individual classes to raise the student-teacher ratio markedly.

There appears to be some justification for this action. Dubin and Taveggia point out that when the relative utility of small classes and large classes (teaching assistants plus high student-teacher ratio) is measured through final examinations, no significant differences are observed. This dilution was begun during the decades when the instructional budgets were constantly rising, and there is now a general feeling that further dilution will seriously hamper learning.

The second option, to delete instruction, could be achieved in two ways. First, total student enrollment could be reduced. Second, courses or whole areas of instruction could be eliminated. There appears to be strong public sentiment, as voiced by elected representatives, against this course of action. Although deletion of students or courses would reduce the total educational budget, there is little evidence that such action would be more efficient in terms of instructional cost per student.

The third option is to develop an improved, more efficient instructional process. The University of California has recently taken three steps that have attracted national attention. One was to reinforce the emphasis on teaching as a major element in faculty activity. Revised criteria for faculty promotions stress teaching performance more strongly, and for the first time explicitly state that the development of new and effective techniques of instruction, which would include recorded instructional materials, should be considered as one of the criteria [Hitch, 1969].

Another step in California was the establishment of a Regent's fund for Innovative Projects in University Instruction. This evidence of administrative interest in developing and improving instruction has met with great faculty enthusiasm, and project proposals coming from all campuses have far exceeded available funds. The fund specifically invites proposals for the innovative development and use of learning resources, although the funds are not limited to that type of proposal.

Another recent step was a set of recommendations for the improvement of undergraduate instruction. The problem of costs was implicit in these recommendations, because they made no mention of increased funds for this purpose. Explicit mention was made of increased allocation of faculty time to undergraduate instruction and the need to survey all ways, including learning resources, for improving its quality [Hitch, 1969].

Dubin and Taveggia support the administrators' attempts to explore the option of development. They suggest that a distinction needs to be drawn between short-term cost savings and long-term cost savings in college instruction. They note that the first option, employing large classes and using cheap graduate assistant instructors, involves short-term savings. They add, "There are available teaching technologies which have long term cost-saving features that may be more beneficial in the long run but which require high level initial investments [p. 50]." They urge continued exploration along this line.

It appears that the majority of administrators, like the majority of teachers and students, are now positively committed to increased use of learning resources during the next two decades. When the push of the explosive current development of new devices such as videotape cassettes, 8mm film loops, and the learner-paced, slide/tape units device is coupled to the above requirements-pull, it is difficult to find good reason to doubt such growth. But this commitment is far from unanimous. Some administrators, teachers, and students across the country appear largely indifferent, and a few others are even actively hostile to learning resources. However, a decade ago, not even a majority were positively committed. This shift in opinion has been so gradual that it has been largely unnoticed until the last few years.

There is perhaps less agreement across the country as to the ends of higher education than there is to the use of learning resources as one means of achieving these ends. In a time of rapid change in our society, a healthy divergence of viewpoints may well be a sign of vitality in higher education, not decay. Such differences should not be allowed to impede the growth of learning resources, because these resources will be needed regardless of which educational goals a campus decides to pursue.

EFFECTIVENESS

Not only does a majority of faculty, students, and administrators agree that learning resources, judiciously employed, can improve instruction, but solid experimental evidence of the effectiveness of learning resources in higher education is accumulating from carefully controlled empirical research. The effectiveness can be demonstrated, even though it cannot be always explained, any more than other parts of the teaching process can. Research on teaching has so far reached the stage of *hypothesis,* a provisional conjecture as to causes and relations of phenomena. This research has not yet produced *theory,* a verified hypothesis applicable to many related phenomena. Gage [1963] points out that the theory of teaching has been neglected while the theory of learning has received a great deal of attention. "Theories of teaching need to develop alongside, on a more equal basis with, theories of learning [p.133] ."

This lack of a theoretical base is regrettable, for, as Kurt Lewin once remarked, there is nothing so practical as a good theory. But this lack can hardly be used as an argument against the development of learning resources. That would be as unrealistic as suggesting that the entire system of higher education be closed down until a comprehensive theory of teaching is developed.

Dubin and Taveggia lay a good share of the responsibility for the failure to develop a comprehensive theory of teaching on those engaged in educational research. They chide their colleagues for devoting four decades to the measurement of student performance on final examinations in the hope of finding that the traditional approach, that is, small-size classes with discussion-type interaction taught in a personalistic fashion, is a superior method of teaching.

> The research literature on comparative college teaching methods is astonishingly clear (indeed, almost unique among behavioral science data in this respect): we cannot claim superiority for *any* among different teaching methods used to convey subject content to the student [p. viii] (emphasis supplied).

Clearly, this research has not contributed to the development of a theory of teaching.

Two final comments by Dubin and Taveggia are pertinent to this discussion:

> We [charge] our research colleagues to make a marked shift in the strategy of doing their research on pedagogy; and [urge] academic policy-makers to broaden the grounds for their decisions on college teaching methods [p. vii] .
>
> . . . any strategy of continued studies of comparative college teaching methods designed to produce a significant pay-off must proceed to examine outcomes . . . other than student performances on final examinations [p. 5] .

The best empirical evidence of the effectiveness of learning resources comes, as Dubin and Taveggia have urged, from studies that measure outcomes other than student performance on final examinations. For example, Blancheri and Merrill [1963] found that television could be used to teach dental technique in 35 per cent less time with no loss in student achievement. Conklin [1970] compared (a) lecture and drill, (b) lecture plus laboratory, and (c) synchronized slide/audiotape presentations in teaching embryology. Although the lecture-drill method was significantly less effective than the other two, the lecture-laboratory method and slide/tape methods did not differ on initial learning or on a subsequent measure of retained learning. This outcome might have been predicted from the findings of four decades of research. However, the slide/tape method took approximately 65 per cent less time than either the lecture-drill or the lecture-laboratory methods. The repeated findings of a significant amount of time saved by the use of learning resources is only one of several research outcomes that merit the confidence of administrators, teachers, and students in higher education.

PRESENT MISCONCEPTIONS

Learning resources should be no more exempt from criticism than are other components of higher education. One type of criticism is particularly justified—that which is directed against inadequate facilities, inferior instructional materials, and incompetent learning-resources personnel. Such inadequacies are exasperating to all and should be corrected as soon as possible. The President's Commission on Instructional Technology stated bluntly in March 1970: "The present status of instructional technology in American education is low in both quantity and quality [p. 21]."

In another type of criticism, mentioned at the beginning of this chapter, learning resources are faulted when the objection is in fact directed against a particular approach to teaching. This type of criticism is particularly difficult to justify within an institution of higher learning.

Three misconceptions about learning resources should be laid to rest. It is unfortunate that such misconceptions are repeated so frequently and die so slowly.

The first misconception is that nothing can be done without further research. This ignores the existence of a substantial body of instructional media research that, as previously indicated, dates back to 1917. Probably the most competent comprehensive review of instructional film research from then until 1950 was made by Hoban and van Ormer [1951]. Summaries of subsequent film studies and all major television studies through 1963 were prepared by Reid and MacLennan [1967]. Perhaps the most incisive analysis of instructional television research findings was made by Chu and Schramm [1967]. One of the better recent summaries of research on teaching machines and programmed instruction is edited by Glaser [1965]. Barnes [1972] has developed an extensive bibliography of computer-assisted instruction. Campeau [1974] summarized the research on the use of a broad range of audiovisual media to teach adults.

In contrast to the amount of research devoted to learning resources, there has been a paucity of experimental research on textbooks. Carpenter (as cited in Lumsdaine, 1963) noted that there were no known experimental comparisons of the effectiveness of alternate versions of text material. In his highly regarded summary of research on teaching at the college and university level, McKeachie stated in 1963 that despite the age of printing as a technique, there is relatively little research on its use [p. 1156]. Those who say that there has not been enough research to justify the use of learning resources should be therefore even more vigorous in their opposition to the textbook.

The second misconception is that learning resources will replace the teacher. It is the dark side of the bright promise that learning resources will free teachers from certain repetitive activities that they would otherwise have to perform, leaving them with additional time for more productive and rewarding activities in the area of teaching. This misconception was first voiced on arrival of the educational motion picture, and it was repeated again and again as television, language laboratories, programed instruction, and the computer were made available to assist in the teaching process. Throughout this period there is no evidence that even one teacher was released because of any of the new educational media. To give even cursory consideration to the personal contribution required of the good teacher in planning, organizing, leading, and controlling instruction is to agree that any teacher who thinks he can be replaced by a machine ought to be. The more that faculty members learn about instructional technology the more they realize the teacher's function transcends that of a machine, and the jest about replacement appears less and less threatening.

The third misconception is based upon the fact that competing brands of a similar item of learning resources equipment are often incompatible, along with other shortcomings, and assumes that some ideal device will soon be on the market if we only have the wisdom to delay. Waiting for the ideal equipment usually produces unfortunate consequences. Not only is nothing done over the short range, so that effective contribution that current equipment could provide is lost, but a massive purchase of the supposedly ideal equipment at some time in the future could be disastrous if an honest mistake is made. The more prudent course is to obtain equipment in stages by purchasing devices that can support the current objectives of high instructional priority. The experience gained from a limited purchase will prove useful if and when additional equipment appears desirable.

SUMMARY

Learning resources have always played a role in instruction conducted in centers of higher education. Learning resources centers here include the facilities, materials, and personnel that directly assist the teacher in his conduct of instruction. During the next decade college teachers will be engaged in testing several major conflicting hypotheses concerning instruction. All these hypotheses assign significant, if somewhat different, roles to learning resources.

Use of learning resources will continue to expand during the next two decades. The majority of students and administrators now agree with the majority of the faculty that more learning resources of some nature are a necessity. Solid empirical evidence of the effectiveness of learning resources supports this opinion. The ever-increasing availability of a wider range of instructional devices contributes to this demand. Three misconceptions interfere with intelligent discussion and planning in this area. The idea that more research is needed ignores literally hundreds of significant studies on the effectiveness of learning resources. The idea that learning resources will replace the teacher ignores the fact that no machine can compete with a good instructor in the complex human interactions essential to effective teaching. The erroneous idea that perfect devices and materials will soon replace the inadequate ones available at present becomes an excuse for doing nothing. It will always be necessary to analyze the capabilities and limitations of learning resources in relation to the objectives of instruction, so that this misconception provides no valid reason for delay.

The expanding use of learning resources in institutions of higher education raises problems of academic and administrative control that have, by contrast, attracted little serious attention. It is these problems and their solution that receive consideration in the following chapter.

Advantages of a Center for Learning Resources

Shortly before his retirement, Edgar Dale, the distinguished professor of education at the Ohio State University, summarized the major issue about the use of learning resources in higher education by stating that some persons discuss learning resources as though there were a real choice as to whether we should introduce them into higher education. That decision has already been made. The only choice that remains is, he added, "whether we use learning resources wisely and plan for them, or whether we use them grudgingly, ineptly, and planlessly [in Curl, 1967, p. 24-25]." Part of such a choice concerns the degree of centralization of learning resources that is planned for on a university campus. The campus administration can decide: to leave learning resources development and management entirely to the individual academic departments; to centralize only certain types, such as educational television; to organize all learning resources under some central system.

In this book, a center for learning resources is defined as *an organized activity consisting of a director, staff, and equipment housed in one or more specialized facilities for the production, procurement, and presentation of instructional materials and the provision of developmental and planning services related to the curriculum and teaching on a general university campus.*

The first organization of visual education in the colleges and universities appeared in conjunction with extension divisions formed in the early 1900s. Expansion of media services to include on-campus activities was a later and overlapping development that dated from the establishment of audiovisual centers in the 1930s and 1940s. As on-campus media services expanded, they were sometimes allied to extension programs and sometimes not [Brown and Norberg, 1965]. The expansion of media services at the University of California is an example of media services developing from a strong alliance with extension services.

Although many major universities in the United States had established centralized facilities for on-campus activities, including television, between 1948 and 1960, that was not the case with the University of California. In support of extension's off-campus activities, an impressive collection of instructional materials and devices had been assembled, mainly motion picture films. On-campus departments of instruction arranged to draw upon these resources and to supplement them with direct departmental purchases.

This arrangement worked reasonably well during the late 1940s and the 1950s because University Extension media activities were centered in Berkeley and Los Angeles. As the University expanded to nine decentralized campuses, this arrangement became increasingly cumbersome for on-campus instruction.

The expansion of Santa Barbara is a case in point. Following the move from the Riviera campus to the Goleta campus in 1954, it became necessary to establish a small audiovisual service as a part of the library. In 1963, Audio-Visual Services moved from extremely limited space in the Library to quarters in the Arts Building. At the same time, the administration established initial provisions for the coordination of Audio-Visual Services and Educational Television Services as a separate entity that has now grown into a full-fledged Office of Learning Resources. Other campuses followed a similar pattern.

In Los Angeles in 1962, the Chancellor established the Academic Communications Facility, which was intended to provide a full range of learning-resources service at no charge to the academic departments for formal on-campus instruction. With the subsequent decentralization of control of University Extension activities to the several campuses it became increasingly difficult to justify the maintenance of separate learning resources facilities for on-campus instruction and for Extension.

As of June 1971, seven of the nine campuses of the University of California had campuswide learning resources centers, if the facilities of the Medical Schools at Davis, Irvine, and San Diego are considered along with the general campus facilities in this category.

The diversity of terminology noted in the previous chapter is illustrated on these seven campuses: each of the learning resources centers has a different name. Yet in the past decade all but two of the Chancellors have found it advantageous to move toward centralization of the service and management of learning resources.

The University of California Libraries do not appear to have played a significant role in the development of learning resources as defined in this report. On only two of the new campuses—Santa Barbara and Santa Cruz—were the new libraries assigned organizational responsibility for learning resources, and this responsibility was subsequently shifted away from them. On all other campuses, the libraries have had little to do with learning resources. One campus has given the following reason for separating learning resources from the activities of its library [Planning Guide for Project 908074, 1969, p. 5] :

> [Non-print instructional materials] differ from library materials in that they are more complex; require specialized production, storage, distribution and display facilities; and depend for their most economical and efficient use on electro-mechanical technologies.

In summary, the expansion of the University precipitated the gradual shifting of learning resources from University-wide Extension to a centralized facility on each campus under the control of the Chancellor. The new campuses tended to establish a separate nonprint learning resources center about as soon as the new campus became operational. The first established campuses to centralize were already maintaining two or more separate campuswide production units, such as photography and television. Centralization on the two other established campuses has not taken place to date.

Thus, the University of California reflects the general movement in higher education toward a greater centralization of learning resources. Erickson [1968] states six broad generalizations for organizing media service programs. The first principle is as follows:

> Principle 1. The work of organizing and developing instructional media services will proceed most effectively under specialized, *centralized* leadership, working coordinately with other curriculum personnel and under adequate *system-wide financial support* for auxiliary staff, equipment, materials, and facilities [p. 22] (emphasis supplied).

The advantages of centralization are also apparent overseas. In Great Britain the University Grants Committee allocates the funds appropriated by Parliament for higher education. In 1963, a subcommittee was appointed to survey the current use of audio-visual aids in teaching and research in the pure and applied sciences in institutions of higher education, to assess their potential usefulness and possible lines of development in Great Britain. Paragraph 435 of the subcommittee's report, *Audio-Visual Aids in Higher Scientific Education* [1965], says.

> The committee recommends large-scale development for the purposes of Higher Education in the use of film, of conventional and new visual aids, of closed circuit television, of programmed instruction and of language laboratories. It recommends that institutions of Higher Education should set up *central units* offering to component departments audiovisual facilities and services; and that these central service units should be linked to a National Centre (emphasis supplied).

It is considered particularly significant that a central unit was judged the most advantageous by representatives of the British instructional system, which is traditionally based on group discussion and tutorials.

ADVANTAGES

A university campus gains three major advantages from establishing a learning resources center. These three advantages are noted in publications on this subject in the United States and abroad. The advantages are savings, improvement of instruction, and institutional coherence.

Savings

As indicated above in the statement by Erickson, a learning resources center is composed of leadership and staff personnel, equipment, materials, and facilities. Centralization of each of these components results in savings.

Facilities savings can be made by providing a special structure for the center. The Project Planning Guide [1969] for the University of California Santa Barbara Learning Resources Center points out that:

> ... such features as the requirements for high ceilings in the television studios, sophisticated electronic systems, and special sound-proofing treatment of many areas can be accommodated with an overall saving in construction and operating costs by concentrating the personnel and facilities in one structure [p. 3].

Additional savings can be obtained by having the central staff operate a facility used by several departments. At many universities and colleges, each language department has developed its own language laboratory operated by its own staff. The central language laboratory facility on the University of California Santa Barbara campus serves up to 5,000 students per week during the Fall quarter of each year, but only uses two non-academic staff members supported by student General Assistance (hourly) help to carry out the full operation, including complete maintenance.

Further savings can be made by reducing the number of large lecture halls, classrooms, and laboratories per campus through effective use of learning resources. The concept of distributing lectures by closed-circuit television to the residential colleges reduces the need for additional auditoriums. The addition of a videotape capability means that a lecture can be repeated several times during a given week, permitting flexible scheduling during any portion of the day to include early morning or late evening hours. For every added class of the same type that needs to be scheduled, the potential savings in instructional staff time amounts to one-third to one-half full time equivalent (FTE). The use of the autotutorial system in an anthropology course at the University of California, Santa Barbara, made it possible to improve student achievement and double the size of the class with no increase in allocation for laboratory space.

It has not been uncommon in some universities for major academic departments or schools to set up closed-circuit television facilities to serve their own purposes. These limited facilities are seldom interconnected except at great cost because of basic design incompatibilities. In contrast, a centralized facility provides a central communications hub for intercampus and intracampus electronic communications—video, audio, and computer—via cable and microwave relay. Not only can a system of campuswide communications be used to produce overall savings, it also can be used to contribute to the coherence of the institution it serves, as will be discussed later.

A center also contributes to savings in equipment, beginning at the time of purchase. For example, all learning resources equipment purchases are carried out through the center. New items are analyzed by the center staff for suitability and dependability prior to purchase. Upon receipt, the items are checked operationally before being placed in service, and preventive and major maintenance procedures are subsequently carried out by the technical staff.

At the University of California, San Francisco, the departments of psychiatry, neurosurgery, nursing, and dentistry have gained a competitive advantage in securing research grants requiring television equipment by working through the Educational Television Division of the campus learning resources center. The Division maintains a list of future research requirements and purchases equipment that is appropriate to a series of investigations. The investigator with a three-year research project may need equipment that has a normal effective life of seven years. Under the San Francisco arrangement the investigator's budget for equipment rental is only three-sevenths as large as the equipment purchase figure on competing grants. At the conclusion of the project, the equipment is put to another constructive use instead of sitting unused, taking up laboratory storage space.

Major savings accrue from the pool of instructional devices maintained by the learning resources center for use by the academic departments. The number of each type of device in stock can be adjusted to the frequency of faculty demand for each type. When a Department of Telecommunications was established at a major Big Ten university some years ago, a check of instructional devices purchased by academic departments was conducted. Among the purchases that had been ordered during the previous five years were a substantial number of opaque projectors. An on-the-spot check in departmental closets revealed that twenty-two of them had never been removed from their shipping boxes! This lack of use represents a dead loss to the university. The center thus achieves equipment savings in three ways: by assisting in the purchase of dependable equipment that fills a *bona fide* instructional need, by operating a pool of instructional devices so that each item has a high level of use, and by scheduling repair and maintenance so that "down-time" is kept at a minimum.

Finally, a center can provide savings in the cost of learning resources personnel. There are two ways by which this savings can be measured. A common measure is to hold the number of personnel constant and to inquire whether a centralized or decentralized approach provides more service. Under decentralization, personnel are frequently "hidden employees." For example, a highly skilled laboratory technician may be commandeered to spend his spare time in a photographic dark room developing negatives and prints on a piece-work basis. There is a triple waste here, because (a) the salary of the laboratory technician is higher than that of a photographic technician who is (b) technically competent to turn out superior work on (c) automated equipment that is far more efficient than manual piece-work techniques.

A preferable measure is based on the type and scope of service that is required by a given campus. Given these criteria, it is possible to determine whether the number of personnel needed is greater under a centralized or decentralized system. Learning resources personnel can be employed more efficiently when all are working together under competent professional supervision. The needs of all departments do not peak at the same time, so that each department gets more competent service from a smaller total number of learning resources personnel. A centralized service is better able to recruit, train, and supervise student help, another means of achieving savings in the cost of personnel.

Centers can also maintain a basic full-time staff to operate an on-going program, but this draws support from part-time student employment during periods of peak campuswide activity, which aids a number of students in financing their educational program and costs the campus less than full-time staff.

Improvement of Instruction

The second advantage of a learning resources center rests in its capacity to improve instruction—one of the major conclusions drawn by Thornton and Brown [1968] :

> Probably the greatest single encouragement to faculty members in improving instruction, and perhaps in achieving the economies that new media promise, will be the ready availability of competent paraprofessional staff, housed in efficient and well-equipped quarters, to assist with the research and preparation of instructional materials that truly effective and creative teaching requires [p. 146].

Faculty members want their teaching to enable students to go beyond the narrow limits of acquiring units of information, measured by the number of hours spent in a classroom. They have added the goals of broadening the students' horizons, liberating them from dogma and prejudice, and giving them that new sense of identity that should characterize the results of a university education.

In a study of what recent college graduates felt were the most significant things that happened to them in college, Sanford [1968] interviewed a bright young alumna who reported two experiences. One occured in a freshman seminar in which the teacher made her feel that what she had to say was being listened to and was a worthwhile contribution to the group. The other experience was in her senior year when a teacher spent a long time pointing out the weaknesses of a difficult paper.

It is not generally recognized that these two memorable teachers achieved this sensitivity through intuition or experience. It was not developed in them through formal training. Most teacher training in schools of education has proceeded on the assumption that teachers are mainly transmitters of information, according to Sanford, and they are accordingly taught the skills needed to pass content from books or personal experience into the minds of the students. To be sure, schools of education produce chiefly elementary and secondary teachers. The average college teacher is even more poorly prepared. Graduate schools, from which college teachers come, pay almost no attention to teaching; they fill their students' time with specialized courses and assume that if they can earn their doctorates, they can teach [Sanford, 1968].

Sanford sees the development of learning resources as a hopeful sign that teaching may eventually be restored to its rightful place: "Teaching machines may show that information can be handed out by means other than the live lecture, and educational television may bring the best lecturers to more students and thus force other teachers to become good discussion leaders, and good tutors, rather than lecturers [p. 171]."

The Commission on Instructional Technology [1970] stressed this same point noting that, as a labor-intensive system, education is growing more expensive without becoming more effective. With the communications media available, it is high time instruction became more productive. If, as seems clear, some of the functions performed by human beings can be performed as well or better through other agencies, teachers could assume versatile, differentiated, human roles in the schools.

There seems little doubt that during the 1970s, learning resources are destined to play a constructive role in helping improve postsecondary instruction—a role based upon the difference between teaching and informing. As summarized by Thornton and Brown [1968]:

> It would appear that today's economic realities in higher education require, above all else, that a proper distinction be made between the acts of *teaching* and *informing*. Making and accepting this distinction is believed to be the first important step toward alleviating some of the problems now facing higher education. Two things seem to be needed: (a) wider understanding of the fact that simple *informing* may often be performed quite adequately (and economically) through the use of materials or the software produced for use in various electro-mechanical devices ... and (b) a better understanding of the fact that, as always, *teaching* continues to require (more than informing) the in-person contributions of professors in illuminating, elaborating, questioning, evaluating, and managing the necessary give-and-take involved in exchange of ideas with students [p. 119].

The typical learning resources center of the 1960s was not fully prepared to assist faculty members directly in improving instruction. The Commission on Instructional Technology noted "our study has shown that one-shot injections of a single technological medium are ineffective. At best, they offer only optional 'enrichment' [p. 7]." Often lacking were personnel skilled in what we currently call *instructional development.* Recognition of this need led schools across the nation to stress instructional development in their learning resource centers. The most successful of these have included persons who are themselves skilled teachers, who have a current knowledge of the findings of educational research, who are competent to assist in the validation of all new approaches to teaching, who have the time to work with instructors in organizing new courses and in reorganizing present courses to make them more effective, and who have the knowledge of when instructional media should be used and when they should not be used.

One major recommendation of this report is that the learning resources center on every campus be supported in acquiring staff members with a similar expertise. The demonstrated success at some medical schools is one of the strongest arguments for the desirability of this improvement.

With the addition of the instructional development unit, one central organization can offer a busy faculty member all the major learning resources for improving instruction. The efficiency and convenience of this arrangement enables the faculty members to make more extensive and effective use of these resources.

There are two compelling reasons in favor of a central facility for the general campus. The first concerns the quality of each component within the center. Learning resources centers include personnel, as well as equipment and materials. Persons qualified to work in particular areas of learning resources will be in short supply throughout most of the decade. Once a high-quality staff is assembled to purchase and produce high quality equipment, materials, and services within a learning resources center, these resources can then be shared by the entire campus on an equitable basis. Quality is also expressed by the range of learning resources available to improve teaching. There are certain expensive production facilities that are needed urgently but infrequently by any single school. A center can supply this service when the combined needs of all schools and departments on a campus make it economically feasible.

The second reason is related to the way in which a center actually functions. A good center created from high quality components improves with time. The principle is crossfertilization. This principle applies within the center itself. After visits to educational institutions that lacked a well-developed learning resources center, the Commission on Instructional Technology concluded that although increasing numbers of classrooms make some use of instructional films, television programs, tapes, records, etc., the exponents and practitioners of the various instructional media operate without sufficient contact, coordination, and crossfertilization [p. 48].

This principle also applies to functional relationships between the center and the on-campus departments. The variety of instructional problems stimulates creative solutions. Conversely, a good solution worked out with one department can be passed along to another department that faces a similar problem. For example, new techniques for measuring student achievement frequently have applications broader than the specific purpose for which they were designed. Another example, from the University of California San Francisco campus, concerns an instructor-operated television teaching desk. Designed to improve instruction in a dental school laboratory, it was found to be equally useful for the visualization of medical school anatomy lectures. It was an alert staff member of a centralized educational television facility who first suggested each application. No person outside the television facility was aware of both teaching problems and the device that could solve them.

This same kind of crossfertilization can make a substantial contribution to the reciprocal stimulation of improved instruction for the full-time on-campus students and for the part-time students in the off-campus degree programs. Self-instructional materials that the center helps produce for part-time students may find useful applications to on-campus instruction, and vice versa.

Institutional Coherence

Most citizens are acutely aware of the increasing rate of change that the United States has experienced during the last 125 years. Few citizens are explicitly aware of the corresponding changes within higher education. Sanford [1968] describes one effect of these changes as follows:

> Inside the universities, life often appears to be every man for himself, with each department, institute, center, or agency focused on its own special interests. One is forced to ask whether there are any general purposes of the whole institution and, if so, who is looking after them [p. 177].

This feeling, Sanford concludes, is not the result of size as such, but lack of coherence. Small institutions, he explains, may lack coherence as often as large institutions do, although the specific reasons are not necessarily the same. In the course of interviewing a large sample of students several times each year during their college careers, Sanford and his colleagues discovered that institutional coherence and the strength of peer culture vary inversely. When faced with fragmentation among the adults, students turn more exclusively to each other, but when shown a larger purpose, they know how to respond [p. 178].

It frequently happens that under extreme conditions a function may be observed that has remained unnoticed in a more conventional situation. One of these extreme situations developed on a University of California campus during the military incursion into Cambodia in May 1970.

The campus had been relatively quiet during previous periods of student unrest and the extraordinary sense of outrage and betrayal felt by the majority of the student body over the Cambodia situation was therefore all the more unexpected. Open student hostility to the campus administration became a factor for the first time, with the faculty in the center of the field of fire. Whether this reaction on the part of the students was justified or not is irrelevant to this discussion. In either case, it was the responsibility of the Chancellor to keep the campus from splitting apart. As Sanford could have predicted, the students turned to each other and organized a mass meeting in their student union building and a breakdown in communication became imminent.

It was not realized until later that the first test of the Chancellor's willingness to enter into a dialog with the students was their request for access to the campus closed-circuit educational television facilities. Both administration and students had grown accustomed to having television involved in events of campus importance, and from that standpoint, the request did not seem unusual. After careful consideration the Chancellor granted the student request, knowing that the students were aware that the television monitor in his private office would enable him to follow their discussions even when he was not present at their meetings. In the end, it is generally agreed, the campus emerged from this potentially disastrous situation with a stronger sense of community and mutual respect than had previously existed. Moreover, there had been no campus violence, and the disruption of regular classes had been minimal.

The idea that a learning resources center may serve as a useful tool in helping a campus community to regain or maintain a sense of coherence is so new that, like many new ideas, it strikes one at first glance as slightly frivolous. No claim is made that this successful outcome was due solely to the campus communication system within the learning resources center. Nevertheless, it is a matter of record that the Chancellor commended the volunteers among the television staff for their important contribution. In retrospect, to paraphrase McLuhan, it seems the willingness to share the medium was the message.

If a learning resources center is to contribute significantly to a sense of coherence, it must do so under normal, as well as extreme, conditions. Sanford has already provided insights as to what some of those contributions may be. By freeing faculty members from some of the time formerly devoted to *informing* students, the center can make possible more *teaching* contact on an individual basis. Sanford's endorsement of the small resident colleges at the University of California at Santa Cruz is based on the existence of a center for learning resources. In these and other ways, it is possible that the current decade will see the learning resources center as symbolic of the dedication of the institution to the fostering of learning by undergraduate and graduate students alike, both on campus and through alternative forms of higher education.

The existence of a center for learning resources on campus does not guarantee savings, the improvement of instruction, or a sense of institutional coherence. These three advantages are not obtained unless the center is properly organized, administered, and supervised. It is these topics that are considered in the chapter to follow.

Administration of the Learning Resources Center 3

The body of research and study is now sufficiently developed to support certain criteria for the administration of a university learning resources center. The existence of this body of information on administration is in itself testimony that the learning resources center has already become an element of some importance in higher education.

It is frequently said that educational administration, like public administration and business administration, is concerned with the solutions to three central problems: management, decentralization, and controls and standards. The university learning resources center is no exception.

MANAGEMENT

The most critical aspects in center management concern services, leadership, and university administrative structure.

Types of Service

The Higher Education Media Study, which was sponsored in part by the U. S. Office of Education, sought data by questionnaire and personal visit from approximately 1,400 of the 2,207 institutions of higher learning established in the United States in

1966. As a result, even though not all contacted institutions appear in the final sample, study directors Thornton and Brown [1968] were in a unique position to report on the current status of management of media services. They found that the concept of on-campus administration of media services has progressed from the original purpose of providing films, projectors, and projectionists to the provision of media-enhanced services to professors and students that have the potential to revitalize and modernize instruction in all departments of colleges and universities of America [p. 144]. Thornton and Brown's findings are supported by other studies, both in the United States and abroad.

The learning resources center in higher education has an obligation to help all members of the faculty who come to it. It must avoid a partisan role in the lively controversy over theories of teaching and be prepared to offer a range of services. For example, it must be as well organized to handle a request for a few slides to enliven a lecture as it is to assist in the preparation of a self-instructional sequence designed to substitute for a lecture.

This obligation implies more than the single passive service role. The modern learning resources center provides five major types of service.

1. The first major type is *production services.* Sub-categories include the preparation and production of: live and recorded television presentations; photographic materials such as prints, slides, and motion picture sequences, graphic materials including art work, charts, diagrams, displays, and exhibits; and self-instructional materials which may require additional production steps. The principal user is the course instructor. This type of service is available in most college or university learning resource centers. This service requires such equipment as cameras, microphones, recorders, and film processors and printers. Space must be allocated for studios, dark rooms, editing rooms, and related acitivtes.

2. The second major type is *group presentation services.* These services include activities that support instructors as they teach groups of students in the classroom, seminar room, or laboratory. Learning resources for this type of service are char-

acteristically employed as aids to instruction. For example, in the case of a motion picture film or sequence of slides, the instructor prepares the class members for what they are to see, may interrupt the presentation to ask key questions, and at the conclusion of the film or slide sequence directs a question and discussion session to make sure the points have been grasped and to give the students practice in applying the principles or concepts just presented. The instructor is present in person to control the situation in which learning is expected to take place. This type of service requires such equipment as video distribution systems and television monitors, playback equipment, projectors, and loudspeakers. Space must be allocated for equipment storage, videotape and motion picture collections, preview facilities, and film booking and maintenance activities.

3. The third major type is *self-instructional presentation services.* These services include activities that support the student as s/he assumes more responsibility for his/her own learning of a unit of instruction. Ideally, the student is under the control of the instructional materials themselves. From them s/he learns what s/he will be able to do after successfully completing the sequence of instruction. From them the student receives information about the subject matter, questions that focus on key points, practices in using and applying the information, and has an opportunity for self-test to gain assurance that s/he can in fact do what s/he set out to learn. This type of service requires instructional materials that differ fundamentally in function from visual aids. These materials are presented in instructional devices specifically designed for use by one or two students. Space must be allocated for student study carrels, computer terminals, collections of self-instructional materials, and equipment maintenance.

The principal user is the course instructor. Self-instructional materials do not relieve the instructor of a responsibility to manage and select learning experiences so that each student has the maximum opportunity to achieve the objectives of the particular course. The self-instructional materials should help the instructor to do so more effectively.

4. The fourth major type is *instructional development services.* These services are provided through consultants employed

by the learning resources center. Instructional development basically involves the identification of specific objectives, the assessment of learner characteristics, the development of learning systems designed to meet the specified objectives, and the evaluation of the learning system as well as of learner progress. These activities all take place within the context of a given content area, course, or program. The principal users are the course instructor and the department chairperson.

The Higher Education Media Study [Thornton and Brown, 1968] noted that learning resources were often available but inadequately used, mostly because faculty members did not feel at ease with them and did not know how to go about applying them to their instructional problems [p. 132]. Organizing and conducting a course of instruction is a complex and difficult task, and every good teacher knows instinctively that the mere use of learning resources is no guarantee of greater success. During the 1960s, and earlier, few learning resources centers employed anyone with expertise in instructional development to stay with one teacher until a particular instructional problem was solved. Brown and Norberg [1965] pointed out that many potentially significant projects have aborted because the interested teacher was not given sustained consultant support.

Some instructional development problems can be solved in a short time, and many problems involving learning resources can be solved without the services of the instructional development consultant. The good teacher or department chairman is most likely to seek out the consultant when s/he is organizing a new course, reorganizing a troublesome unit within a course, considering a more innovative approach to a given subject area, or evaluating the effectiveness of an existing course. This type of service requires no equipment for the consultant other than a typewriter and desk calculator. No space is required other than a private office within the learning resources center.

Thornton and Brown [1968] stated that in the whole field of administration of new media, this may be the area of greatest future potential [p. 132]. Their prediction is rapidly coming to pass. At the National Conference of Directors of Biomedical Communication in 1971, 32 of the 68 learning resources centers represented employed consultants in instructional development.

There are similar indicators of such growth in Peterson's man-power studies [1974, 1975, 1976] , the growth of AECT's Division of Instructional Development, and the increasing amount of professional literature devoted to instructional development. The provision for at least one consultant in instructional development as a full time employee of the learning resources center staff is recommended as a planning criterion.

5. The fifth major type is educational *planning services.* These services are provided by the director and the senior staff members of the learning resources center. The principal users are the dean of a school or college and the chairman of an academic department. These services include cooperative planning to insure that all necessary learning resources are available for the support of existing school and departmental curricula, to determine learning resources requirements for proposed changes in the curriculum, to prepare equipment and facilities specifications for new building construction, and to insure an appropriate budgetary balance between learning resources and other aspects of the school and departmental instructional program. These services require no special equipment. No space is required other than regular offices and a conference room.

Of the five major types of service, the effective delivery of educational planning services is the least written about and the least understood. It is actually a new problem generated by the development and promise of instructional technology. Deans and department chairmen are thus not yet sure which are the crucial questions involved in this kind of educational planning, and the directors are not yet sure what constitutes a competent answer. In addition, the machinery by which this dialog might take place has not even been formally established on many campuses. For example, the standing procedure seldom calls for the dean and the director of learning resources to meet jointly when the instructional program of the school is under review.

Vigorous efforts to solve the substantive and precedural aspects of this problem may well result in the discovery and elimination of obstacles that prevent optimum use of available learning resources. Criteria are seriously needed in this area. The identification of such criteria is one of the crucial developments to be accomplished in the decade ahead.

Leadership

Thornton and Brown [1968] discovered in the course of the Higher Education Media Study that all five major services are handicapped by management deficiencies. The full potential of technology to improvement of college teaching can be realized only through instructional *planning.* College and university media services directors seldom play significant roles in analyzing goals and designing strategies to attain them. "The administration of media services has become," they say, "in all parts of the nation, an exercise in instructional *leadership* [p. 144]" (emphasis supplied).

Thornton and Brown list certain qualities the director of the learning resources center must possess if s/he is to provide his/her share of such leadership. The director should be oriented primarily toward the improvement of college teaching rather than to the mere management of media facilities. S/he should have general competence in matters pertaining to curriculum improvement, and s/he should be skilled in working with those faculty interested in improving their teaching.

> The head of the audiovisual services or instructional resources should be a professional member of the faculty who merits respect and acceptance from the rest of the faculty. Competent and well-meaning though he may be, the young technician who is seen by the faculty simply as a distributor of materials and repairer of equipment will have a difficult time promoting innovation [p. 131].

Thornton and Brown thus place the criterion of leadership near the top of any list of planning criteria for the university learning resources center. The director of the center should be selected according to standards that correspond to those applied in the selection of the rest of the faculty. One important traditional standard is academic preparation. This standard has not been applied to directors in the past because a generally accepted program of relevant academic preparation simply did not exist.

It was not until 1955 that academic programs in 50 colleges and universities justified the publication of the first *Directory of Graduate Programs for the Professional Education of Audio-Visual Supervisors, Directors, and Building Coordinators.* Most of these programs were at the master's degree level and oriented toward elementary and secondary education. The most recent directory in the series, prepared by Larson, is *Instructional Technology Graduate Degree Programs in U.S. Colleges and Universities, 1969-71.* At least 35 U.S. universities offer doctoral programs in the theory and management of learning resources. These programs qualify the doctoral candidate to work in learning resources at the level of higher education. A typical program includes rigorous work in learning theory, educational psychology, systems design, curriculum theory, communications, and administration.

U.S. universities are paying increasing attention to the standards of academic preparation. Edgar and Sims [1970] reported that 87 per cent of the U.S. directors in their survey have advanced degrees, compared with 62 per cent of the Canadian, 32 per cent of the United Kingdom, and 25 per cent of the Australian directors. This percentage, while encouraging, requires qualification. Many of the doctoral degrees are not specifically related to learning resources. However, Peterson's studies [1974, 1975, 1976] show an increasing number of graduates of advanced programs going into administration of media services and into higher education.

These data are not meant to imply criticism of any university learning resources center director who lacks such preparation. As in the selection of other faculty members, academic preparation is only one of several standards applied in decisions on selection and promotion. Experience and proven abilities should be carefully considered. Thornton and Brown do, as mentioned earlier, state that academic preparation is also a great asset for a director, especially in dealings with the faculty.

The management of learning resources for the benefit of higher education is now a recognized field of study. Graduates of these programs are now available. The number of universities that have appointed these graduates to positions of leadership is rapidly increasing. The provision for a director who is qualified according to high standards of academic preparation as well as experience is recommended as a criterion for planning the university learning resources center.

University Administrative Structure

The most appropriate administrative structure is the one that best facilitates the functions that the organization is designed to perform. Key structural factors are the level of placement of the director, the relationship with the library, and the internal organization of the learning resources center itself.

In educational administration, the so-called "unit type" of organization is generally accepted as the desirable pattern. One person, the chief administrative officer, is responsible for the total educational enterprise, including the instructional program and its related business or financial affairs. Brown and Norberg [1965], in their book *Administering Educational Media,* state that the organization of media services is usually similar: one person has full responsibility for the program, including the development and administration of the departmental budget. They add that this arrangement is desirable and consistent with the notion of centrally coordinated planning of all media services. The University of California is an excellent case in point. Like most major U.S. universities, it is organized on the unit type of pattern. The logical development of nine separate campuses to serve each of the major clusters of population within the State made a strongly centralized administration within the Office of the President undesirable. Accordingly, the responsibility for the administration of each campus was delegated, within certain limits, to the Chancellors, who became the chief campus administistative officers.

To employ a University-wide director of all learning resources would have been inconsistent with the general policy of delegated authority. Thus, each Chancellor was given authority over almost all aspects of the instructional program on his campus, including learning resources. A University-wide position of Director of Educational Television was phased out in the mid-1960s, and the development of campus-wide centers for learning resources, as described in the preceding chapter, began to grow.

The unit type of learning resources center organization appears to be moving toward a very high percentage of adoption. Writing in 1965, Brown and Norberg state that this was the "usual" pattern. By 1970, according to the Edgar and Sims survey, unit type of responsibility for planning control, allocation of funds, and decisions on services had been given to directors in more than 70 per cent of the U.S. universities in the sample [p. 22], indicating strong preferences for unit type administration.

Level of Director Placement. In his book, *Administering Instructional Media Programs,* Erickson [1968] states that placement of the media program director in an administrative organization is a vital matter. Leadership, decision making, design and planning activity, responsibility, all part of the total capacity for change, are some of the vital factors involved [p. 27].

Erickson recommends that the media director should be placed at the highest possible point in the administrative and institutional hierarchy that permits him/her to work coordinately with other leaders, but under direct authority of the chief decision maker. S/he should be in a position to focus all of his/her energy and effort on the media development program. This recommendation is extremely important. It recognizes that the university administration must provide leadership and support at the highest level if the learning resources center is to operate effectively. Thornton and Brown agree with Erickson that "the faculty director of instructional resources ordinarily should report directly to the institution's chief academic officer, rather than to the dean of any of the schools of the university [p. 131]." Heinich, author of *Technology and the Management of Instruction,* is on record that ". . . instructional development should enter at much higher levels of the administrative hierarchy [Stowe, 1971, p. 36]." Ramey [1971] states this point as follows:

> Acceptance of the departmental director as a peer of the professional staff is the most critical factor, but it is almost as important to have the operation initiated by someone at a level high enough in the organization to give it unquestioned administrative and professional sanction from the beginning. Lacking these factors, the operation is typically perceived as a low-level, low-priority service function that really has little to do with the mission of the organization [p. 97].

Erickson's recommendation also recognizes the interdependence of learning resources with other elements of the instructional program. His emphasis on a coordinate level with other leaders points up the twin dangers of placing the director at a level that is too high, as well as too low, for effective operation of the learning resources center.

In view of the importance that most authorities give to the proper location of the learning resources center within the university administrative structure, a recommendation in this regard is more than justified. Therefore, the following criterion is recommended as most appropriate: the director of learning resources should report to the chief *academic* (level two) officer on each campus.

Relationship with the Library. Emergence of the learning resources center has stimulated a number of articles on its relationship with the library. There is general agreement among the authors that this relationship is an important one and should be strengthened. The director of a library serving a general campus should be recognized as a coordinate leader of instruction along with the deans of academic schools and colleges and the director of a campuswide learning resources center. All three types of budget should be considered together for their appropriate contribution to the instructional program.

A few authors have gone further, suggesting that the library and the learning resources center might best prosper from presenting a united front based on the merger of print and nonprint media. Such an organization would control a basic "commodity," the management of information and its dissemination [Hamlin and Sprinkle, 1971]. One means of assessing the extent of this commonality is to consider the five major types of service expected of a learning resources center. What existing skills and competencies of the library can be drawn on to enhance the service?

Specific commonalities are fewer than might be expected. Most libraries have little experience with production services, a distinguishing characteristic of the university learning resources center. They have no experience in the important new area of instructional development services. It is possible that the library could make procedural contributions in educational planning services. Library budgets have been in general more stable in recent years as indicators than those of learning resources centers. On the positive side, self-instructional and group presentation services could benefit greatly from improved systems of cataloging, one of the central skills of the library. There is good evidence that provision of some self-instructional media study space in the library is eminently feasible [Merrill, 1970]. However, there is also good evidence that limiting *all* self-instructional media use to the library is undesirable [deGroot, 1970].

Careful studies of merged media activities, and even reports of such operation, are rare. Miller [1970] tested on secondary school teachers the hypothesis that audiovisual use would become more respectable if associated with the library. A unified media program seemed to produce no better audiovisual climate than separate audiovisual programs.

The *Drexel Library Quarterly* devoted an issue to Issues and Problems in the Management of Nonprint Media. The editors solicited an article from the university director of a merged media facility for the health sciences. Merging apparently resulted in no new form of organization: each half of the organization chart is prepared as if print and nonprint activities operated independently, up to and including separate faculty advisory committees. This merged facility has separate circulation desks and storage areas for print and nonprint media in order to exercise the requisite controls over the nonprint collection [Hamlin and Sprinkle, 1971].

James W. Ramey, professor in the Graduate School of Library Science at Drexel University, points out a current difficulty with such proposed mergers.

> The plain truth of the matter is that most librarians are book oriented and plan to stay book oriented if they possibly can. Placing a book oriented librarian in a media center doesn't change the librarian. Unfortunately, all too often it does change the media center [p. 95].

This condition can change, and schools of library science and graduate degree programs in instructional technology should give it greater attention. There is room for additional experimentation, despite the fact that there are leanings in the opposite direction. The crucial question, it would seem, is whether or not the campus instructional program, including the extension and alternative programs, is best served by a merged print and nonprint media facility or by separate facilities.

Internal Organization. The nine-campus survey of the University of California (described in Chapter 4) by the writer included a request for the organizational structure of the learning resources center. None of the centers was organized in exactly the same fashion, yet each structure could be explained in relation to local campus operational problems and the amounts and types of service called for. We conclude that no single pattern of internal organization can satisfy the varying needs of all campuses. Accordingly, no criterion model is recommended for the current decade. Each campus should have the flexibility to tailor the center's internal organizational structure to correspond with its unique requirements.

Although no criterion model is recommended, an acceptable organizational chart should include the following. The director should report to the chief campus academic officer, and all five major types of service should be provided for. An example of how a health sciences campus center is organized to accomplish these requirements is shown in Figure 1. Whether or not such an organizational pattern can be applied to a general campus depends on the identification and analysis of the unique needs of such a campus.

DECENTRALIZATION

A learning resources center with a large and varied clientele must be ready to adjust general policies and standards to diverse local or specialized circumstances; yet too great a latitude may make effective general action difficult or impossible and lead to distortions that may injure the general good. On the other hand, specialized knowledge should be employed if a program is to be wisely administered. A learning resources center must recognize the circumstances that indicate physical as well as administrative decentralization.

Physical Decentralization

What size is "large" for a learning resources center? This question was particularly important for the University of California, which in 1968 had campuses ranging from just over

Figure 1
Vice Chancellor—Academic Affairs
Communications Office for Research and Teaching

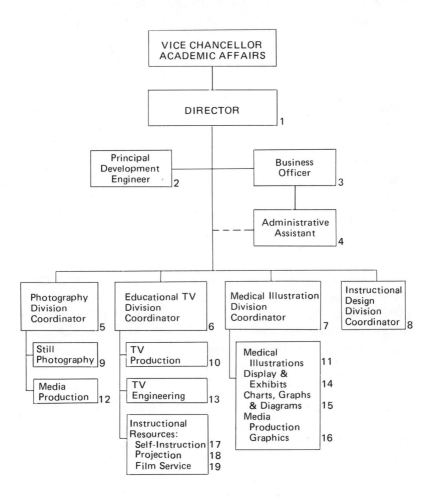

Major types of services provided by units and offices:
  A. Production: 9, 10, 11, 12, 14, 15, 16
  B. Group Presentation: 13, 18, 19
  C. Self-Instructional Presentation: 17
  D. Instructional Development: 8
  E. Planning Services: 1, 2, 3, 4, 5, 6, 7, 8

1,000 to 27,500 students. At that time, the learning resources center directors agreed that, as a rule of thumb, a single building designed to house learning resources facilities might serve a campus of 15,000 students, but that when enrollment exceeded that number some geographical separation for certain activities was mandatory; and some separation might be desirable even for smaller campuses.

The directors reported that such decisions are made according to the standard measures of educational efficiency: does this type of decentralization make instruction more effective at the same cost in time and/or money or does it provide equally effective instruction at less cost in time and/or money? When these measures are used, physical decentralization tends to be selective. On one campus, television recordings are produced and copied in a well-equipped central studio and the copies are distributed to several campus locations where inexpensive playback equipment has been installed. On another campus, motion picture and slide projectors and audio tape recorders are serviced in a centralized repair shop, but they are then returned to several locations that are readily accessible to faculty members, where they are checked out when needed for instruction. On a third campus a language laboratory facility is established in a location that is separate from that of the other learning resources facilities because all user academic departments are clustered around the former location.

Administrative Decentralization

In the above examples, the learning resources center was in full control of these learning resources activities even though they occurred in physically separate locations. Physical decentralization can thus take place without administrative decentralization, which is often defined as the dispersion or delegation of functions or powers from a central authority to regional or local governing bodies.

In some instances administrative decentralization should accompany the geographical separation of learning resources [Newman, *et al.,* 1971]. The Newman report states: "While coordination, rational planning, and the elimination of waste are important goals, centralization is often pursued in areas where its benefits are illusory [p. 26] ." There is also danger in the opposite extreme. The nine-campus survey discovered that one University of California campus has 22 separate instructional television installations, none of which is coordinated with the central television facility. What is needed is a reasonable policy that avoids the extremes of overcentralization and fragmentation.

The nine-campus survey found that no learning resources center of the University of California reported having a policy on administrative decentralization that indicated the general conditions under which it should occur. It is probable that the centers are still too new to have gained sufficient experience to justify establishment of such a general policy. This situation is not limited to the University of California. Edgar and Sims reported that in most universities in the Australian, British, Canadian, and American sample, audiovisual services are provided by either one or several other departments as well as by the audiovisual centers. They add, "This duplication is viewed rather ambiguously by the centers [p. 25] ." Hooper [1969] in analyzing reasons for the failure of educational technology cited the fractionation of various media and empire building, especially at the college level [p. 253] .

In many cases, decentralization revolves around highly specialized techniques—for example, ophthalmic photography. The technique is restricted to use by a single, professional school and requires specialized equipment and training in its use. However, employees of this unit may be on the staff of the learning resources center, which serves as a source of recruitment and promotion, vacation replacement, technical support, and business management supervision. Direct supervision of the employees as they do ophthalmic photography would be delegated to the faculty member who reviews their work for its contribution to patient diagnosis, to scientific data, and to instruction of medical residents.

The preceding example concerns the successful decentralization of a specialized production service. An example of the decentralization of a group presentation service is on a decentralized campus with residential colleges. Recruitment and daily supervision of a student work crew is delegated to each residential college because these crews perform other duties for the colleges in addition to audiovisual support. The learning resources center trains the students, maintains the equipment they operate, and provides other back-up services as required. In this case the center reimburses the colleges for the time devoted to audiovisual activities. The advantage of this decentralization results from more efficient use of crew time and a single channel of supervision.

These are only two examples of administrative decentralization where special situations dictate the wisdom of decentralization. In other circumstances, the center may wish to delegate to a dean the authority to appoint and supervise all senior staff members of a special unit for his school. The unit's duties may go beyond learning resources, and the authority to support directly certain elements of the program. The chancellor may wish the center to retain full responsibility for over-all campus planning and for serving as a source of recruitment and promotion, technical support, learning resources equipment inventory control, and to share with the dean the responsibility for planning the learning resources needs of the school. Provision for administrative decentralization along some such lines appears preferable in the long run to attempting to manage two fragmented operations that each require substantial budgetary support.

CONTROLS AND STANDARDS

Complex systems function through the simultaneous operation of a set of subsystems, and the system of higher education is very complex indeed. Just as the subsystems of the human body require control and regulating devices, so the healthy function of the body of the university requires that its educational, research, and service subsystems must operate according to appropriate controls and standards.

What standards should apply to a learning resources center? Learning resources are an identifiable component of the educational system, along with such traditional components as the students, the teachers, the academic setting, and the budget. In general, each of these components must be controlled and regulated so that the educational objectives of the university are achieved effectively and, it is hoped, efficiently.

One of the important practical results of the federally supported regional laboratories for educational research and development has been the discovery of a model that provides for such controls and standards. Through trials, reevaluations, and subsequent corrections, dramatic improvement in instructional effectiveness was found to depend on the specification, development, and integration of five program systems. Baker and Schutz [1972] identify them as instructional system, training system, installation system, accountability system, and modification system and the authors describe them as they relate to a particular course or sequence of courses. We suggest that they apply equally as a basis for campuswide planning. These program systems are partially operational on all of the nation's campuses; they are completely designed and fully operational only on a few of them.

Each of the five program systems is described below in terms of its contribution to the campus educational system. Included in each description are one or more illustrations of the contribution of the learning resources center to that specific program.

1. The *instructional* system is the most obviously necessary program. It consists of all the methods and materials that have been prepared to accomplish specified instructional goals. It includes everything needed by the user to achieve specified learner outcomes, and it provides the bases for specifying the requirements of all other program systems. This system specifies what learning resources must be produced by the center and in what quantity. It specifies the group and self-instructional presentations that are required. The instructional development unit of the center is involved, along with teachers, students, administrators, and budget and space specialists, in the design of this program. Learning resources production and presentation requirements then become operating objectives of the center.

2. The *training* system has been all too frequently omitted on most campuses. It includes the materials and procedures required to train teachers and others responsible for the support of instruction. A good course, or a good degree sequence for that matter, must be maintained for several years to be of real instructional value to the institution. It takes that long to attract the students who can benefit from it, to develop a faculty

who can contribute to the field, and to justify the expense of creating an attractive and excellent program. Faculty turnover must be anticipated. Training in the application of improved instructional strategies must be provided for professional advancement in addition to upgrading junior faculty members through sabbatical leaves, seminars, and national conferences. Too many outstanding courses that make use of innovative techniques deteriorate because the replacement teacher has not been trained in their use. The learning resources center should be required to provide such instruction on a continuing basis. This training requirement then becomes an operating objective for the center.

3.   The *installation* system is often characterized by insufficient planning. It consists of the procedures and materials required by a user to introduce and install an instructional program effectively. It pertains to administration, including functions and personnel having authority and responsibility for supervisory, curriculum, and learner personnel services. Many innovative programs have withered because of lack of appropriate administrative support. Procedures were not modified to accommodate the new program, it was not explained sufficiently to gain general acceptance, it was not provided reasonable space, or staff and financial support, etc. An appropriate installation system specifies learning resources that are required in the new instructional program, states the extent of the new requirements and provides sufficient lead time for their development, and insures that the center budget is adequate to carry out such activities. The center provides data on which administrative decisions can be based and collaborates in the establishment of new procedures necessary to install the new instructional program. Specific installation requirements then become operating objectives of the center.

4.   The *accountability* system is the primary source of controls and standards. It includes all the mechanisms required to maintain maximum student proficiency and the procedural adequacy of the above instructional, training, and installation systems. The assignments and responsibilities for which personnel will be held accountable are anchored to specified program

and/or procedural outcomes. The system includes the collection of the data required to assess the outcomes for which accountability is to be maintained. The center is accountable for achieving its instructional, training, and installation objectives, as are the other components of the educational system, and operating data are collected that permit assessment of its performance objectives. Center staff members are held accountable for their individual performance as specified by this system.

5. The *modification* system provides for a program of evaluation and improvement. It includes all the procedures, materials, and strategies required to analyze the operations of the above system, to detect specific limitations, and to effect improvements in program and performance. It includes rules for correcting deviations in operation and provision for documenting identified sources of system breakdown, override, and remediation. Too frequently a curriculum is abandoned when it "isn't working," and a totally new one is designed, because administrators and teachers had never agreed on what would constitute evidence of system breakdown and what workable procedure would be used for modification. The research and evaluation skills of the center are used in developing this system in collaboration with others. Procedures for modification of center activities, as well as of other components of the educational system, are included in this program system.

Truly adequate standards for a learning resources center cannot be established without reference to the standards that apply to the other components of the educational system, and the standards for all components must be derived from the goals of the campus educational system. The five-program systems model provides a conceptual framework that is broad enough and specific enough for the eventual accomplishment of this important task. A competent learning resources center can be of substantial help to a campus in developing these five program systems, because the center uses this expertise daily in its instructional development activities.

The following chapter presents data on learning resources staff and space requirements that are necessary to support a wide variety of instructional system programs.

Criteria
for Staff
and Space

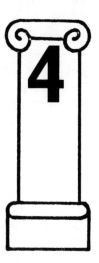

The specific purpose of this chapter is to present criteria for staff and space allocations to the learning resources center of a general campus. The criteria are appropriate to the current and future needs, can be applied to several levels of student enrollment, can be adjusted to the unique instructional program of each campus, and allow maximum flexibility to campus planners. The criteria suggest answers to planning questions such as:

How many persons, for example, are required to operate a photographic production service of minimum scope for a campus of 5,000 students?

What floor space is required for basic studio production of television presentations for a 15,000-student campus?

How many people are required to operate a learning resources center on a 1,000-student campus?

Answers to these questions are critical in both planning and operations. Administrators need them as a guide for supporting the current instructional program and for future planning. Funding agencies need them as a guide for operating budgets, which are centered around the staff, and for capital outlay budgets for remodeling or new construction, which are based in part on requirements for space. Faculty members need these answers as a reassurance that they are guaranteed sufficient resources to reorganize a course sequence or to develop instructional material.

A comprehensive set of criteria governing allocations of staff and space within the university learning resources center has been sadly lacking. Elementary and secondary schools have been more fortunate. The need for guidelines for federally funded programs for the development of the new media led the American Library Association and the National Education Association to the joint publication of *Media Programs: District and School* (1975). An original version (1966) of these guidelines of this nature did include a reference to higher education. The later editions in 1969 and 1975 dropped this reference. Joint guidelines (AECT-AACJC-ALA, 1973) exist for media programs in 2-year postsecondary institutions. However, there are no guidelines for 4-year institutions—colleges and universities.

Compliance with these elementary and secondary school standards—and to some extent, the 2-year college standards—will have an important impact on higher education. Students arriving at college will be accustomed to a far greater use of learning resources than was the case in former years. Typical recommendations for elementary and secondary schools of 500 students are as follows: filmstrips, 500-2,000 items; 16mm films and Super 8mm sound films, access to 3,000 items; audiorecordings (tape and disc), 1,500-2,000 items.

Media Programs: District and School is based on previous editions and on the consensus of a distinguished group of experts. They have been well received and widely used. However, there is no research that ties the standards directly to the elements of an instructional program. There are no means of objective verification of the recommendations to support a proposed change in the instructional program. While AECT has developed a media program evaluation based on the standards and is currently field testing the evaluation documents, there is no objective verification of the links between media program and instructional program. There is no rationale or formula from which to calculate new requirements for media to support a proposed change in the instructional program. In elementary and secondary education, where instruction is usually predicated on students mandated to attend classes in large, continuous (and contiguous) time periods (in the daytime) from Monday through Friday, a generalized approach to media programs may suffice. The general approach probably covers the majority of instructional programs and changes can be made on an ad hoc basis. In higher education, attendance is no longer involuntary; time periods are brief and often not contiguous; classes are more likely to be held in the evening than in K-12; classes have more opportunity for variation in type of instruction. In higher education, there is more opportunity for the instruction to come to the student instead of the student coming to a single central location for class—even though the opportunity may not be used.

It should be obvious that no single standard can reasonably be applied in higher education since colleges and universitites also vary widely in size, in subject matter of instruction, and in the interests and backgrounds of the student bodies.

At the university level, one direct link between the wide variation in academic programs and criteria for instructional space and staff is *student learning time.* Student learning time is defined as the total time that a student devotes to his courses, including time spent in class, in the laboratory, and in individual study. For a portion of this learning time, the student is under the stimulus and reinforcement of one or more kinds of learning resources. Naturally, the extent of this portion affects the amount of learning resources support the center is required to supply. The campus that plans to have 20 per cent of student learning time involving learning resources will need a center with more staff and space than a campus that plans to have only 1 per cent of student learning time occupied in this manner. While there may be other links between instruction and criteria for staff, space, and resources, student learning time (as defined above) is a significant variable understood by professor, administrator, developer, and resources planner alike. Student learning time is also amenable to further use in studies of the effectiveness and efficiency of instructional techniques.

Student learning of academic subject matter occurs effectively both in a traditional classroom setting and outside it, and learning resources have been found to be effective under certain circumstances in all these learning situations. The California legislature has recently recognized that calculations based solely on time spent in the traditional classroom fail to do justice to the instructional program in higher education. The law now provides that the state include in the computation of average daily attendance for community college districts the time that the students spend in programs using "television, computer-assisted instruction, automated audio-visual systems, programmed learning techniques, and other similar teaching techniques," even though the classroom teacher is not providing immediate supervision. This type of instruction is termed an Approved Coordinated Instruction Systems Program.

The analysis of student learning time has broad utility. It is essential in computing staff and space criteria for the campus learning resources center, and it can be extremely helpful to the Extended University as courses are developed to serve both on-campus and part-time students. The amount of learning time required for successful completion of a course is a crucial consideration for the student who must schedule his instruction around full- or part-time employment. Furthermore, student learning time is a unit of measure that permits the logical articulation of the input of all coordinate elements of instruction, including the teaching faculty, the library, and the learning resources center.

The criteria were designed to allow maximum flexibility to campus planners. Flexibility is particularly important, because criteria that become straightjackets are almost certainly counterproductive at this early stage of learning resources center development. The criteria in this book were developed from existing program information (beginning with the University of California at San Francisco) and then reviewed and subsequently approved by the learning resource directors at each University of California campus. There is sufficient variation among campuses to indicate that results of the development study are generalizable to a large number of colleges and universities.

DEVELOPMENT OF THE CRITERIA

The criteria apply to a general campus, using the University of California as a model. A *general campus* is one that offers degrees at the baccalaureate, masters', and doctoral level in a wide variety of subjects through a number of colleges. The criteria are not intended to apply to elementary and secondary schools, to community colleges, and to advanced education in professional schools such as medicine and law. That does not mean the criteria will not work—only that they still must be reviewed and tested in these areas.

The criteria were designed to include four independent variables: type of service, scope of service, enrollment, and percentage of learning time. Definitions of these variables along with amplifying comments are as follows:

Type of service—production, group presentation, self-instructional presentation, instructional development, planning—was defined in the previous chapter. Because they differ in staff and space requirements, the following Subtypes of production services were considered separately: television, photography (including motion pictures), graphics, and programed instruction. Two Subtypes of Group Presentation Service were added for the same reason.

Scope is defined as the range of the activities offered within each Type and Subtype of service. The minimum activity that can be justified as a campuswide service is designated as Scope A, and the maximum activity that is justified as Scope D. Using the Subtype, television production service, as an example, Scope A is limited to activities requiring inexpensive portable television equipment for live magnification in classroom and laboratory and for the recording of micro-teaching exercises. Scope D (the broadest scope) includes full studio production activities using color television. Scopes B and C represent intermediate points in the range of activities that can be conveniently identified. Note that Scopes B, C, and D are cumulative and each includes the activities of all lesser Scopes; for example, Scope B includes A, Scope C includes all of Scope A and Scope B.

Enrollment is categorized in terms of four levels, using 1,000 students as a practical minimum. This level provides an excellent baseline for extending data to the larger campuses. The second level of 5,000 students is currently approximated at the Irving, Riverside, San Diego, and Santa Cruz campuses of the University of California. The third level of 15,000 students is now being approached by the campuses at Davis and Santa Barbara. The maximum level of 27,500 students has been reached at both Berkeley and Los Angeles. Use of these levels enhances the validity of the criteria, because the University has practical operating experience at each level upon which to draw. The calculations for this variable take into account the fact that a greater variety of academic subjects is usually offered as the level of student enrollment increases.

Percentage of Learning Time is defined as the percentage of total student learning time during which the student is under the stimulus of learning resources. All space and staff criteria data presented in this chapter are based upon the calculation of 10 per cent of learning time. This figure is now generally accepted as most useful for planning purposes. The Carnegie Commission (1972, p.1) predicts a figure of between 10 and 20 per cent of on-campus instruction and up to 80 per cent or more for off-campus instruction by the year 2000.

The dependent variables of the design are expressed in terms of Full Time Equivalent (FTE) for staff and Assignable Square Feet (ASF) for space. The University of California uses these terms for planning and analysis that involve staff and space. The terms are defined as follows:

FTE is defined as one person employed in the appropriate job full time, or the equivalent, which may be made up of a combination of part-time persons, skilled or unskilled, staff or student employees.

ASF is defined as the sum of all floor space that can be assigned to center activities, including space for repair and maintenance areas, waiting rooms, and storage closets as well as for dark rooms, and studios. It does not include adjacent space for public hallways and toilets, for example. ASF for a single room is usually considered as the space located between the principal surface of the walls and partitions at or near floor level.

The above design produces a matrix of 288 individual cells that accounts for the effect of the independent variables upon staff and space. (Developing the cells from specific activities required 696 individual estimates.) The datum entered for each cell is an estimate based on expert judgment. A tentative estimate was prepared for each cell by the Communications Office for Research and Teaching at the University of California, San Francisco. Learning resources personnel on the other campuses then reviewed the estimates on the basis of their experiences in their settings. The final estimates presented in this chapter have been approved by center directors on all campuses of the University of California.

Those involved in producing the tentative estimates were instructed to proceed as follows: first, estimate ASF and FTE for each Type and Subtype of service at Scope A (the minimum) for a student enrollment of 1,000; second, extend estimates through Scope D for 1,000 enrollment; third, extend all Scope A estimates successively to 5,000, 15,000, and 27,500 enrollments; and fourth, extend Scope B in the same manner, followed by Scopes C and D. This procedure was adopted in order to begin with an established minimum and to provide at least one base line for every incremental estimate. Those involved in reviewing the tentative estimates were instructed to begin with cells that described services currently offered on their own campuses.

This methodology was adopted to increase the confidence that may be placed in the accuracy of the criteria and to provide a means of objective verification. Greater confidence can be placed in a final figure that results from summing a series of estimates, each of which deals with a limited set of conditions for which current experience data are available. Planners would rather examine how the FTE and ASF needed for each Type and Subtype of service contribute to the total requirement than to be presented with a single estimate of the total FTE and ASF required.

Objective verification can be obtained by a census or survey of student learning time. The individual course is recommended as the unit of measure. Such a survey can yield data of the type shown for Chemistry 1A, as a hypothetical example (Table 1).

Table 1
Student learning time under learning resources
and other stimuli for Chemistry 1A (sample)
for one week of instruction.*

		Student learning time					
		Resources Stimulus		Other Stimuli		Total Stimuli	
Activity	Materials	(min)	(%)	(min)	(%)	(min)	(%)
Lecture	2 charts 15 slides** 1 film (16mm)	40	33	80	67	120	100
Laboratory	1 programed text	40	13	320	87	360	100
Individual study	2 VT recordings**	60	25	180	75	240	100
	Total	140	19	580	81	720	100

*A 4-unit course: 2 hours lecture, 6 hours laboratory, and 4 hours individual study per week. Percentage of Learning Time: 19 per cent.

**Produced locally.

The percentage of learning time for the entire campus instructional program is obtained from course data weighted according to enrollment. Group and self-instructional presentation services requirements are obtained from time devoted to the materials listed. Production services requirements are obtained from the number of materials and presentations produced locally. The information grouped by courses yields data for the planning services provided to departmental chairpersons and deans.

In the absence of widespread verification, the criteria are open to further review. However, changing the total for a single cell does not invalidate the matrix as a whole. The appropriate change must be suggested for the individual cell, presenting evidence that the number is too small or too large, modifying the previous estimate.

RESULTS OF CRITERIA DEVELOPMENT

The results of this study are considered in terms of general and specific findings. Four of these general findings suggest important considerations in staff and space planning that are frequently overlooked or not understood.

General Findings

1.   There is no standard or typical learning resources center size that is appropriate for all general campuses. Table 2 indicates that at 10 per cent learning time the number of employees of the center may range from a maximum of 146 FTE to a minimum of 12 FTE. In terms of space for 10 per cent learning time the range is also very broad: from 45,976 ASF at the maximum to 3,689 ASF at the minimum. How these figures vary if the percentage of learning time differs from 10 per cent will be considered later. A mental stereotype of a standard campus learning resources center can often lead planners to assumptions about cost or placement of such centers that they would not make if a detailed analysis of campus needs were computed according to the procedures indicated in applying the criteria (page 61).

2.   As campus enrollment increases, the ratio of learning resources center staff FTE/student and the ratio of learning resources ASF/student decrease. However, this relationship is not linear. A 27,500-student campus does *not* require 27.5 times as many FTE as a 1,000-student campus. Table 3 indicates that this finding holds true for every Scope (A-D) of service. Planners should not assume that doubling the enrollment of a 15,000-student campus means doubling the staff and space of the learning resources center to maintain existing services at their present Scope.

Table 3

FTE/student and ASF/student ratios according to enrollment
for Scope of Service

Scope \ Students	1,000 FTE	1,000 ASF	5,000 FTE	5,000 ASF	15,000 FTE	15,000 ASF	27,500 FTE	27,500 ASF
A	0.012	3.7	0.004	1.2	0.002	0.6	0.001	0.5
B	0.027	6.7	0.007	2.0	0.003	1.0	0.002	0.8
C	0.050	11.7	0.013	3.5	0.006	1.7	0.004	1.2
D	0.076	18.4	0.018	5.0	0.008	2.4	0.005	1.7

Table 2
Summary of Staff (FTE) and Space (ASF) Requirements.

Services	Scope	1,000 students		5,000 students		15,000 students		27,500 students	
		Staff	Space	Staff	Space	Staff	Space	Staff	Space
Production									
Television	A	2.5	1000	4.5	1125	7	1875	8	2500
	B	6	1600	3	1925	13	3275	15	4300
	C	11	2200	13	2825	20	4575	22	5800
	D	16	2600	18	3225	27	5575	30	6800
Photography	A	1	350	2	660	4	990	5	1370
	B	5	1306	6	1885	9	2640	12	3570
	C	12	3906	13	4880	15	6030	18	7430
	D	21	8551	23	10005	28	12200	34	14550
Graphics	A	1	375	2	625	3	940	4	1250
	B	2	725	4	1375	6	1990	8	2650
	C	4	1375	8	2775	12	3990	16	5250
	D	6	1625	10	3125	16	4690	21	6150
Programed Instruction	A	1	90	1	90	1	90	2	175
	B	2	160	2	160	2	160	3	245
	C	3	230	3	230	4	300	5	385
	D	4	300	4	300	5	370	6	455
Group Presentation									
Television	A	1.5	200	2	400	8	500	3.5	600
	B	2	300	3	600	4	800	4.5	1100
	C	4	600	6	1400	11.5	2800	14.5	3700
	D	4	600	6	1500	12	2900	15	4000

Table 2 (cont'd)
Summary of Staff (FTE) and Space (ASF) Requirements.

Services	Scope	1,000 students Staff	1,000 students Space	5,000 students Staff	5,000 students Space	15,000 students Staff	15,000 students Space	27,500 students Staff	27,500 students Space
Projection, Audio and Film Rental	A	1	200	3	330	5	510	8	700
	B	3	700	5	1085	8	1770	12	2400
	C	6	1250	8	1860	12	2970	15	4125
	D	12	2100	14	2960	16	4470	20	6200
Self-instruction Presentation									
Self-instructional Units	A	1	764	2	1892	3	3584	4	5276
	B	2	964	3	2092	4	3784	4	5476
	C	2	964	3	2092	4	3784	4	5476
	D	2	1064	3	2192	4	3884	4	5576
Instructional Development									
Instructional Development	A	1	100	1	100	1	100	2	200
	B	2	200	2	200	2	200	3	300
	C	3	300	3	300	4	400	5	500
	D	4	400	4	400	5	500	6	600
Internal Planning and Administration									
Internal Planning and Administration	A	2	610	3	700	3	700	4	1015
	B	3	730	4	820	4	820	5	1135
	C	5	940	6	1030	6	1030	7	1345
	D	7	1150	8	1240	9	1330	10	1645
TOTALS									
All Services	A	12	3689	20.5	5922	30	9289	40.5	13086
	B	27	6685	37	10142	52	15439	66.5	21176
	C	50	11765	63	17392	88.5	25879	106.5	34011
	D	76	18390	90	24947	122	35919	146	45976

3. As the Scope of the learning resources center service increases from minimum to maximum the center FTE/student increases approximately five-fold and the center ASF/student increases approximately four-fold, if any level of student enrollment is held constant. Planners should evaluate this hard fact in terms of the potential contribution of the center to the total campus educational program. Doubling the center staff from Scope A to Scope B may triple or quadruple the usefulness of the center in terms of the variety of each type of service involved. Some academic departments already using the limited Scope A services will also make use of the Scope B services, and other academic departments that could not use Scope A services will find Scope B services of prime utility. In fact, the decision to increase the Scope of any type of service should be based on a survey to determine whether such justification of the increase exists. This justification can exist at every level of enrollment. There is no reason for a planner to assume in the absence of such data that a 27,500-student campus should operate at Scope A.

4. No single FTE-to-ASF ratio can be applied to all the learning resources center buildings on general campuses. Planning for some other types of campus building may be facilitated by having a general rule of thumb that relates the number of staff members to the amount of space they need to work in. In this instance the lack of a general ratio is no handicap because planners now have the specific criteria for space and staff that are presented in the tables to follow. The application of these criteria is considered later.

Specific Findings

Specific answers to the questions posed at the beginning of this chapter are found in Tables 4-12. The following answers also indicate how the tables are to be read:

2 FTE are required to operate a photographic production service of minimum scope for a campus of 5,000 students (Table 5, Scope A, 5,000-student column).

1,400 ASF are required for basic studio production of television presentations for a campus of 15,000 students (Table 4, Scope B, 15,000-student column).

12 FTE are required to operate a modest learning resources center on a 1,000-student campus (Table 2, Totals, 1,000-student column).

The separate computations of staff and space for varying conditions of instruction are presented in the individual cells related to the major types of service in the following tables:

Table

1. Production Services
   a. Television 4
   b. Photography (including
      motion picture). 5
   c. Graphics 6
   d. Programed Instruction. 7

2. Group Presentation Services
   a. Television 8
   b. Projection, Audio, Film
      Rental 9

3. Self-instructional Presentation
   Services 10

4. Instructional Development
   Services 11

5. Planning Services. 12

APPLICATION OF THE CRITERIA

The criteria for staff and space have little value unless the user follows the proper procedure in their application, places student learning time in the proper perspective, and considers the advantages and disadvantages of a learning resources center building.

The first step in the application of the criteria is to examine the total instructional program of the campus. Ideally, this too should lead to a statement that specifies the contribution of each of the coordinate elements of instruction, including learning resources, to the total program. The precise extent of the contribution is less important than insuring that the nature of the contribution is specified. Failure to do so makes rational planning for learning resources impossible.

The second step is to select the types of service required by the above specifications. These decisions concern primarily the Production and Group Presentation Services, because the other types, as indicated in the previous chapter, are clearly necessary in the coming decade. For example, one campus may not require the capacity to produce programed instruction materials because they can be purchased. Another campus program may not require the capacity to produce its own graphics. Most campuses require all four Subtypes of Production Service, but none should be selected unless clearly justified by the specifications of the total instructional program.

The third step is to select the appropriate Scope of each of the services. For example, in regard to Production Services, one campus might require television at Scope A at the same time that it requires photography at Scope C. It is also possible that a type of service may be basically Scope B yet include a Scope C or even a Scope D function. Here again, the specifications of the instructional program are the determining factor. The advantage of the criteria is that they permit such flexibility.

It is important to note that this procedure ties the selection of Type and Scope of Service to the needs of the particular campus. Type and Scope are not affected by the size of the campus. It is possible that a 1,000-student campus might require all selected services at Scope D, whereas a 27,500-student campus might be at an overall average of Scope B. Thus, a small campus with a Scope D production service might be called upon to produce materials for statewide use in the Extended University, which need not invariably look to the large campuses for such support.

Scope is also useful in determining intermediate phases. If a campus 10-year plan calls for the instructional development service to be at Scope D at the end of the decade and no service is currently available, it may be wise to begin at Scope A or B. On the other hand, if a Scope D service is urgently needed at present, a leisurely progression through Scopes A to D is probably undesirable.

Educational planning services provided by the center should be staffed at a Scope that is equal to or greater than the average Scope of all other services. That is particularly important during

Table 4
Television Production Services.

Scope	Services	1,000 students		5,000 students		15,000 students		27,500 students	
		Staff	Space	Staff	Space	Staff	Space	Staff	Space
A	Live & recorded lab production.	1	500	1.5	500	3	750	3	1000
	Micro- & mirror-teaching exercises.	0.5	375	1	375	1.5	625	2	750
	Single-room magnification.	1	125	2	250	2.5	500	3	750
	Total—Scope A	2.5	1000	4.5	1125	7	1875	8	2500
B	Scope A	2.5	1000	4.5	1125	7	1875	8	2500
	Basic studio production.	3.5	600	3.5	800	6	1400	7	1800
	Total—Scope B	6	1600	8	1925	13	3275	15	4300
C	Scope B	6	1600	8	1925	13	3275	15	4300
	Full studio production.	3	400	3	600	5	800	5	1000
	Large auditorium production for multi-section classes.	2	200	2	300	2	500	2	500
	Total—Scope C	11	2200	13	2825	20	4575	22	5800
D	Scope C	11	2200	13	2825	20	4575	22	5800
	Remote production.	2	—	2	200	2	200	2	200
	Quad production, edit, and duplicate.	1	200	1	200	2	300	2	300
	Color production.	2	200	2	200	3	500	4	500
	Total—Scope D	16	2600	18	3225	27	5575	30	6800

Table 5
Photography Production Services.

Scope	Services	1,000 students		5,000 students		15,000 students		27,500 students	
		Staff	Space	Staff	Space	Staff	Space	Staff	Space
A	Copying of charts in black and white for prints (smaller than 10 in.).	1		2	125	4	127	5	255
	Copying of materials for slides (outside processing).		120		120		250		375
	Public relations photography.				55		125		125
	Limited amount of darkroom printing (bulk done outside).		230		360		488		615
	Total–Scope A	1	350	2	660	4	990	5	1370
B	Scope A	1	350	2	660	4	990	5	1370
	Processing of black and white films.		272		375		500		600
	Reception of work and record keeping.		100		125		175		200
	Printing of black and white prints up to 11 x 14 in. size.		286		350		425		600
	Copying of charts in black and white for prints (up to 24 in.).		198		250		400		500
	Simple location still photography.		100		125		150		300
	FTEs required for activities.	4		4		5		7	
	Total–Scope B	5	1306	6	1885	9	2640	12	3570

Table 5 (cont'd)
Photography Production Services.

Scope	Services	1,000 students		5,000 students		15,000 students		27,500 students	
		Staff	Space	Staff	Space	Staff	Space	Staff	Space
C	Scope B	5	1306	6	1885	9	2640	12	3570
	Specimen and photomicrography.		240		280		320		360
	Simple motion picture production.		1360		1560		1760		2000
	Large copy work (any size).		500		575		650		750
	Custom slide mounting (glass, plastics, composites).		200		230		260		300
	ID photography.		300		350		400		450
	FTEs required for activities.	7		7		6		6	
	Total—Scope C	**12**	**3906**	**13**	**4880**	**15**	**6030**	**18**	**7430**
D	Scope C	12	3906	13	4880	15	6030	18	7430
	Color film processing.		1120		1205		1410		1630
	Color printing.		225		250		300		340
	Photomicrography.		300		350		400		450
	Complete motion picture production.		1700		1900		2300		2700
	Major location still photography.		1200		1300		1600		1800
	Reception and film file.		50		60		80		100
	Administration.		50		60		80		100
	FTEs required for activities.	9		10		13		16	
	Total—Scope D	**21**	**8551**	**23**	**10005**	**28**	**12200**	**34**	**14550**

Table 6
Graphic Services.

Scope	Services	1,000 students		5,000 students		15,000 students		27,500 students	
		Staff	Space	Staff	Space	Staff	Space	Staff	Space
A	Drawings, lettering (hand or transfer) for posters, notices, etc. Signs, matting, framing cutting. Supplies and storage.	1	188 125 62	2	375 125 125	3	564 188 188	4	750 250 250
	Total—Scope A	1	375	2	625	3	940	4	1250
B	Scope A Mechanical lettering (LeRoy, Wrico). Drawings, diagrams, charts, and graphs for photographic reporduction. Artwork for duplication (brochures, booklets, etc.). Displays.	1	375	2	625	3	940	4	1250
	Supplies and storage. FTEs required for activities.	1	100 100 150	2	150 300 300	3	200 400 450	4	200 600 600
	Total—Scope B	2	725	4	1375	6	1990	8	2650

Table 6 (cont'd)
Graphic Services

Scope	Services	1,000 students		5,000 students		15,000 students		27,500 students	
		Staff	Space	Staff	Space	Staff	Space	Staff	Space
C	Scope B	2	725	4	1375	6	1990	8	2650
	Headliner.		50		100		150		200
	Composing machine (such as Varityper).		50		50		100		100
	Reproduction equipment (visual aid printer, copier, etc.).		50		100		100		200
	Exhibits.		100		300		400		400
	Models.		50		100		150		200
	Supplies and storage.		50		150		200		300
	FTEs required for activities.	2	300	4	600	6	900	8	1200
	Total—Scope C	**4**	**1375**	**8**	**2775**	**12**	**3990**	**16**	**5250**
D	Scope C	4	1375	8	2775	12	3990	16	5250
	Photostat machine.		50		100		200		300
	Silk screen equipment.		50		100		200		300
	Plastic models.								
	Animation.		150		150		300		300
	FTEs required for activities.	2		2		4		5	
	Total—Scope D	**6**	**1625**	**10**	**3125**	**16**	**4690**	**21**	**6150**

Table 7
Programed Instruction.

Scope	Services	1,000 students		5,000 students		15,000 students		27,500 students	
		Staff	Space	Staff	Space	Staff	Space	Staff	Space
A	Assist faculty members in production of language laboratory audiotapes. Duplicate audiotapes for individual use. Carry out brief assignments for faculty members in the production of graphic self-instructional materials.	1	90	1	90	1	90	2	175
	Total—Scope A	1	90	1	90	1	90	2	175
B	Scope A							2	175
	Accept assignments for as long as 4 weeks to work with a faculty member in rounding out instructional materials for difficult programed courses.	1	70	1	70	1	70	1	70
	Total—Scope B	2	160	2	160	2	160	3	245

Table 7 (cont'd)
Programed Instruction.

Scope	Services	1,000 students		5,000 students		15,000 students		27,500 students	
		Staff	Space	Staff	Space	Staff	Space	Staff	Space
C	Scope B Assist educational psychologist for instructional development to produce graphic self-instructional materials for completely designed course.	2	160	2	160	2	160	3	245
		1	70	1	70	2	140	2	140
	Total—Scope C	3	230	3	230	4	300	5	385
D	Scope C Assist educational psychologist for instructional development to produce program for computer-assisted instruction.	3	230	3	230	4	300	5	385
		1	70	1	70	1	70	1	70
	Total—Scope D	4	300	4	300	5	370	6	455

Note: This service consists of the supply of liaison personnel between faculty and production facilities of television, photography, and graphics. As the scope of this type of service increases, so must the production skills of the liaison personnel to be added.

Table 8
Television Presentation Services.

Scope	Services	1,000 students		5,000 students		15,000 students		27,500 students	
		Staff	Space	Staff	Space	Staff	Space	Staff	Space
A	Single-classroom videotape retrieval.	1.5	200	2	400	3	500	3.5	600
	Total—Scope A	1.5	200	2	400	3	500	3.5	600
B	Scope A	1.5	200	2	400	3	500	3.5	600
	Cable TV distribution to 4–6 general assignment spaces.	.5	100	1	200	1	300	1	500
	Total—Scope B	2	300	3	600	4	800	4.5	1100
C	Scope B	2	300	3	600	4	800	4.5	1100
	Cable TV distribution campuswide.	1	60	1.5	200	2	400	2	600
	Helical Scan VTR loan service.	.5	120	1	400	3	900	4.5	1200
	Vidicon camera loan service.	.5	120	.5	200	2.5	700	3.5	800
	Total—Scope C	4	600	6	1400	11.5	2800	14.5	3700
D	Scope C	4	600	6	1400	11.5	2800	14.5	3700
	ITFS (2500-MHz) linkages with other campuses.	—	—	—	100	.5	100	.5	300
	Total—Scope D	4	600	6	1500	12	2900	15	4000

[NOTE: Table 9 appears on pages 72-73.]

Table 10
Self-instructional Units.

Scope	Services	1,000 students		5,000 students		15,000 students		27,500 students	
		Staff	Space	Staff	Space	Staff	Space	Staff	Space
A	Provide individual student study facilities with a wide range of materials (audio, 8mm films, slides, TV, teaching machines, language training, small group study rooms, programed texts. Collect and catalog materials in cooperation with faculty. Supervise operation and assist student utilization.	1	764[1]	2	1892[2]	3	3584[3]	4	5276[4]
	Total—Scope A	1	764	2	1892	3	3584	4	5276
B	Scope A	1	764	2	1892	3	3584	4	5276
	Central control center to transmit study material.	1	200	1	200	1	200	1	200
	Total—Scope B	2	964	3	2092	4	3784	5	5476
C	Scope B	2	964	3	2092	4	3784	5	5476
	Automatic dial-access system.	—	—	—	—	—	—	—	—
	Total—Scope C	2	964	3	2092	4	3784	5	5476
D	Scope C	2	964	3	2092	4	3784	5	5476
	Computer-assisted instruction.		100		100		100		100
	Total—Scope D	2	1064	3	2192	4	3884	5	5576

[1] One 8 x 8 ft. study room, 20 carrels.
[2] Three 8 x 8 ft. group study rooms, 60 carrels.
[3] Six 8 x 8 ft. group study rooms, 120 carrels.
[4] Nine 8 x 8 ft. group study rooms, 180 carrels.

Table 9
Projection, Audio & Film Rental Services.

Scope	Services	1,000 students		5,000 students		15,000 students		27,500 students	
		Staff	Space	Staff	Space	Staff	Space	Staff	Space
A	Loan service for audiovisual equipment (pool).	1	100	3	200	5	350	8	500
	Limited projection service.		100		130		160		200
	Total–Scope A	1	200	3	330	5	510	8	700
B	Scope A	1	200	3	330	5	510	8	700
	Projectionist service.		100		200		350		500
	Sound recording service.		100		130		160		200
	Film rental and booking (no permanent library).		100		125		150		200
	Maintenance and minor repair of equipment.		200		300		600		800
	FTEs required for activities.	2		2		3		4	
	Total–Scope B	3	700	5	1085	8	1770	12	2400
C	Scope B	3	700	5	1085	8	1770	12	2400
	Rental of films, ordering, cleaning, repairing, and screening.		300		400		500		800
	Maintenance and minor equipment repair.		200		300		600		800
	Complex projection services.		50		75		100		125
	FTEs required for activities.	3		3		4		4	
	Total–Scope C	6	1250	8	1860	12	2970	16	4125

Table 9 (cont'd)
Projection, Audio & Film Rental Services

Scope	Services	1,000 students		5,000 students		15,000 students		27,500 students	
		Staff	Space	Staff	Space	Staff	Space	Staff	Space
	Scope C								
	Film library.	6	1250	8	1860	12	2970	16	4125
	Audiotape duplication.		250		400		500		700
D	Major projector repair.		50		50		100		200
	Off-campus projection service.		300		350		500		700
	Production services for programmed presentations (multimedia).		50		50		100		125
	FTEs required for activities.	6	200	6	250	4	300	4	400
	Total—Scope D	12	2100	14	2960	16	4470	20	6200

[NOTE: Table 10 appears on page 71.]

Table 11
Instructional Development Service.

Scope	Services	1,000 students		5,000 students		15,000 students		27,500 students	
		Staff	Space	Staff	Space	Staff	Space	Staff	Space
A	Offer general consultation to all faculty members on media effectiveness, course construction, and test development. Advise director on internal planning related to improved faculty support by the learning resources center.	1	100	1	100	1	100	2	200
	Total—Scope A	1	100	1	100	1	100	2	200
B	Scope A	1	100	1	100	1	100	2	200
	Consult and assist with experiments to improve the effectiveness of instruction (requires person with considerable expertise in statistics and experimental design).	1	100	1	100	1	100	1	100
	Total—Scope B	2	200	2	200	2	200	3	300

Table 11 (cont'd)
Instructional Development Service

Scope	Services	1,000 students		5,000 students		15,000 students		27,500 students	
		Staff	Space	Staff	Space	Staff	Space	Staff	Space
C	Scope B Provide detailed consultation with faculty committee on design of a single course, integrating all appropriate techniques of instruction with relevant educational methods.	2	200	2	200	2	200	3	300
	Coordinate with programed instruction production liaison assistant as well as faculty member and evaluate course effectiveness. FTEs required for activities.	1	100	1	100	2	200	2	200
	Total—Scope C	3	300	3	300	4	400	5	500
D	Scope C Offer short course in techniques of university-level instruction to new faculty members.	3	300	3	300	4	400	5	500
	Extend consulting service to computer assisted instruction. FTEs required for activities.	1	100	1	100	1	100	1	100
	Total—Scope D	4	400	4	400	5	500	6	600

Note: This unit is devoted to applied educational psychology. At Scope D it offers a full service of test development, practical research studies, and course construction. It is oriented toward faculty needs and is not concerned with administrative problems such as classroom utilization, instructor workload, etc.

Table 12
Internal Planning and Administration.

Scope	Services	1,000 students		5,000 students		15,000 students		27,500 students	
		Staff	Space	Staff	Space	Staff	Space	Staff	Space
A	Manages learning resources center that averages Scope A overall. Provides secretarial assistance to all divisions of center. Seeks outside consultation on engineering and technical problems, as well as problems relating to budget, purchases, and accounts.	2	610	3	700	3	700	4	1015
	Total—Scope A	2	610	3	700	3	700	4	1015
B	Scope A Manages learning resources center that averages Scope B overall. Coordinates engineering and technical development problems between divisions of center and assists in design and planning of media use in new buildings.	2	610	3	700	3	700	4	1015
	FTEs required for activities.	1	120	1	120	1	120	1	120
	Total—Scope B	3	730	4	820	4	820	5	1135

Table 12 (cont'd)
Internal Planning and Administration

Scope	Services	1,000 students		5,000 students		15,000 students		27,500 students	
		Staff	Space	Staff	Space	Staff	Space	Staff	Space
C	Scope B Coordinates business aspects of learning resources center, including purchasing, accounting, and administration of research grants.	3	730	4	820	4	820	5	1135
	Manages learning resources center that averages Scope C overall. FTEs required for activities.	2	210	2	210	2	210	2	210
	Total–Scope C	5	940	6	1030	6	1030	7	1345
D	Scope C Manages learning resources center that averages Scope D overall.	5	940	6	1030	6	1030	7	1345
	Manage facilities of learning resources center that can be decentralized for greater efficiency. FTEs required for activities.	2	210	2	210	3	300	3	300
	Total–Scope D	7	1150	8	1240	9	1330	10	1645

the coming decade. A harrased center director and staff are of little use to faculty, departmental chairpersons, deans, and the chief academic officer when teamwork is required to solve instructional problems during a period of budgetary austerity.

The fourth step is to compare the current enrollment with that projected for 1990, or a span approaching fifteen years. The number of center staff FTE and the ASF should be selected for each annual operating budget on the basis of current enrollment, but plans for space construction or allocation should be related to future needs, particularly for production services, which frequently have special architectural requirements. A television studio requires a greater-than-average ceiling height to accommodate lighting equipment. It must also isolate external sounds. If a 5,000-student campus is scheduled for a 15,000-student maximum enrollment by 1990, it might be more economical to construct the television studio needed to serve the expanded needs. Such a studio would serve present needs and save the cost of remodeling or additional construction.

Anticipation of future requirements was part of the broader vision that dictated the construction of the learning resources center building on the Santa Cruz campus of the University of California. The total ASF to serve a 15,000-student campus were included in the building as constructed. Space of a conventional nature not currently needed for learning resources has been assigned to other activities on a temporary basis. As enrollment increases, permanent space for the other activities will be constructed in phases, permitting the learning resources services to expand in step with enrollment.

Planners should consider decentralization as an aspect of future learning resources needs. Increased enrollment does not always call for more space in the main learning resources center building for each type of service. Space for storing and distributing equipment for group presentations, such as motion picture and opaque projectors, may perhaps be best provided away from the main building at new locations that are convenient to areas of maximum use.

The fifth step involves the data in Tables 4-12. With priorities established according to the requirements of the campus instructional program, it is then a matter of selecting the data on FTE and ASF from each specified cell to arrive at the total requirements of staff and space for the learning resources center.

The criteria state that the number of FTE indicated in a given cell is sufficient to perform the activity specified, including maintenance and repair. The duties of each individual are to be specified by the director according to needs that are unique to the particular campus. In the same manner, it is left to the director to decide, for example, whether ASF for television studio production are to be used for one large studio or two smaller ones.

Learning resources center directors will find the criteria especially helpful in evaluating their own staff and space requirements for a particular Type or Subtype of Service. In certain instances, the local situation may call for more FTE or ASF in a given cell than are indicated. In other instances, a smaller number may be required. The director should be permitted to exceed the criterion in a specific cell, provided that there is an adequate justification.

The chief campus academic officer and planning officers at higher levels will find the criteria of chief value in their review of the total FTE and ASF requested.

These criteria apply to the total services supplied by a campuswide learning resources center, regardless of whether or not they are physically or administratively decentralized. However, some additional staff and space will be required if the decentralization does not follow the lines recommended in Chapter 3. If separate schools and departments also independently develop their own learning resources facilities, the total ASF and FTE on campus devoted to this purpose will be considerably greater because of the inevitable duplication that results.

Percentage of Learning Time

Two questions about percentage of learning time were raised by reviewers of this study. Some learning resources center staff members felt they were doing a good job in responding to all current faculty requests for service with fewer FTE and ASF than indicated in the criteria. What is the significance, they asked, of this discrepancy? A probable answer is that the campus is making effective use of learning resources, but that it is doing so for less than 10 per cent of a student's learning time—a bit below the progress expected on a national basis. Campus planners have the flexibility of selecting a percentage of learning time appropriate to the local educational program and which may lie above or below this norm. Valid reasons that explain the chosen percentage should be offered.

The other question has come from faculty members who inquired whether 10 per cent (or any other percentage) is expected to apply automatically to every course. The criteria carry no such implication. Some courses in the social sciences already have as much as 51 per cent of student learning time in this category (Fagan, 1971), and the instructor would not be asked to reduce this amount. The hypothetical example of Chemistry 1A (Table 1) shows a science course already at 19 per cent. Other courses now have little or no percentage in this category and may require none. The figure of 10 per cent was selected as the average percentage that might reasonably be anticipated in the coming decade for all students enrolled on the general campus.

Thornton and Brown conclude their Higher Education Media Study of 1968 with the comment that no permanent and lasting effect in improving instruction through the application of new media will occur until there is a substantial instructional commitment to this purpose. They state that this commitment must include at least four elements (p. 146):

(a) administrative involvement expressed in financial support and in recognition of faculty participation, by means both of released time and of promotional policies;

(b) adequate capital investment in both space and equipment;

(c) technical staff to assist instructors in development of materials and in operation of technical equipment, with leadership of faculty status and with enough workers to complete requested work within a minimum time; and

(d) faculty interest in improving the quality of instruction.

The Carnegie Commission (1972, p. 89) states that this commitment should lead to goals that are possible and needed. The goal of 10 to 20 per cent of student learning time by the year

2000 represents a proportion of instruction that the Commission considers significant.

Housing the Center

There is, of course, more to housing a learning resources center than determining requirements for ASF. It is significant that Thornton and Brown discuss housing in their chapter on management. Although they feel it impossible and unwise to try to recommend any special facility as a model for all institutions, they make the following statement (p. 132):

> In colleges that provide adequate administrative and budgetary support for improvement of teaching, there is likely to be at least one area in which several related media functions are housed. Thus, a single building may include self-instructional space and learning programs, films, slides, recordings, tapes, maps, charts and diagrams, audiovisual equipment and services for all campus classrooms; facilities for storage, maintenance, and repair of this equipment; photographic services, including microphotography, aerial photography, and film and print processing; graphic arts services; and consultative service in planning new physical facilities to provide for all such new media utilization.

Housing, they stress, affects both the attitude and performance of the learning resources staff (p. 132):

> At several of the institutions visited, new media services were housed in basements of the oldest buildings on campus, or in "temporary" buildings dating from decades ago. On the other hand, the highest morale of staff as well as the more imaginative uses were discovered more frequently on those campuses where unified services were housed either in the library or learning resources center or in connection with one of the special facilities that made extensive use of new media.

Thornton and Brown summarize by listing several rather clearly defined steps that seem essential in any institution that desires to encourage expanded and improved use of new media as a part of its drive toward excellent instruction. The step related to housing is stated as follows (p. 132):

> A convenient and attractive space for the division of instructional services is very important in encouraging faculty acceptance and utilization of these services.

The criteria presented in this chapter are designed to facilitate the general planning for staff and space and to allow for variations to suit local needs. The next chapter makes the transition from staff and space to the financial procedures and budget needs to support them.

Planning the Budget of the Learning Resources Center

Over $3 million was spent in 1970-71 by all the University of California Learning Resources Centers for salaries, supplies, and equipment.* Of this total, approximately $1.7 million was funded directly in learning resources center support budgets. At present, no information is available regarding how much has been spent for learning resources not produced by the centers. A considerable amount is produced within academic departments or purchased directly from outside vendors. However, the amount spent through the learning resources centers alone is a good indicator of the increasing importance of the use of learning resources. The amount also raises the question, "How practical is it to continue such uncoordinated activities without including them all in the overall planning procedure?" Although there may be benefits in administrative decentralization, *all* learning resources facilities and uses on each campus should be considered in school and campuswide budget planning.

*Approximately 1.5 per cent of the total University of California Instruction and Research (I & R) Budget for 1970-71, based on I & R Budget from all sources, not just University General Funds. Compared to the recommended criterion of 10 per cent of student time involved with learning resources, the cost of learning resources is, at present, most reasonable, even if the use of learning resources were to average out closer to 5 per cent, a most conservative estimate.

PLANNING

Which comes first, the budget or the operational plan? If Webster's definition is applicable and a budget is nothing more than a "financial statement of income and expense for a period of time; or, a plan for financing, based on such a statement," then planning would seem to follow the dictates of the budget. The meaningful learning resources center described in the preceding chapters would have great difficulty meeting its objectives if it were constrained in its planning by this dictionary definition. An appropriate generalization, often quoted but not credited, is that "a budget is a plan for the future expressed in dollars." Hartley (1968, p. 6) defines an educational budget as "a financial expression of the objectives, programs, and activities of a school system." This point of view, that proper planning and coordinated activity precede and determine the budget statement, is the foundation of this chapter.

Analytic Tools

There is a long recognized need for analytic tools with which administrators can effectively develop, implement, evaluate, and modify long-range programs. In recent years such tools and techniques have been developed. They include systems analysis, cost-effectiveness and cost-benefit analysis, and the Planning-Programming-Budgeting System (PPBS). These techniques provide a means to undertake the problems of planning, budgeting, and evaluating.

Systems analysis is a means of identifying and ordering the various components of a system and their interrelationships. This helps the decision maker isolate alternatives and determine their consequences. Essentially, systems analysis is concerned with identifying objectives, determining how they can be realized most efficiently and effectively, and recognizing when the objectives have been achieved.

Cost analysis is used to help in choosing among alternative procedures through which the objectives can be reached. Cost-effectiveness techniques are best applied where costs and effects can both be measured in dollars and a direct causal relationship between the two is evident. Effectiveness is therefore determined by measurable physical events. One example is comparison shopping for the identical product where the only determinant is direct cost. Cost-benefit analysis is the broader category. It includes cost-effectiveness, but also includes outcomes that are less explicitly defined or less readily measured. Such factors as enjoyment, recognition, or status may be of considerable importance but are extremely difficult to measure and quantify precisely. Cost-benefit analysis *does* allow for consideration of a greater range of alternatives.

All effective outcomes may not be beneficial, and all beneficial outcomes are not necessarily effective. Effectiveness implies short-term goals and is usually used to minimize cost relating to some specific requirement, or to maximize performance where cost is limited. Cost-benefit outcomes need not be as immediate or as detailed. For example, full consideration can be given to factors other than dollar cost in deciding which of several instructional program alternatives is most cost-beneficial for the university to purchase. An important factor might well be that the students enjoy using one program and dislike another, although learning achievement is the same for both.

The Planning-Programming-Budgeting System (PPBS) sets out to answer the problem of how to choose and implement programs and how to organize and utilize human and nonhuman resources in order to realize identifiable and reasonable objectives, considering the level of finances available.

Not all problems lend themselves to this sort of analysis, and at best, results are only approximate, since PPBS deals with the future and is based on estimates. Properly used, however, it can serve as a means for organizing information as a basis for rational decisions. "The goal of the analysis is not to provide the planner with the alternative that 'maximizes' specific characteristics; the goal is to provide information which together with the judgment of the planner permits a compromise among the characteristics of the alternatives within the various environmental constraints, such as budget level or political atmosphere." (Carpenter and Haggart, 1970, p.6.)

Components of a Good Plan

A good program plan would include the following written components:

specific overall goals and objectives of the total organization with reference to precise time periods;

identification of the goals and objectives of the various programs which comprise the total organization plan;

purpose of each program and how it relates to the total plan;

evaluation process to be used in determining program success;

alternative procedures by which objectives can be reached;

itemized presentation of the estimated cost of each of the alternatives;

bases to be used in determining which of the alternatives would be most effective *and* efficient;

indication of how and when evidence of accomplishment of objectives will be gathered and presented;

definition of the responsibility of the various participants for achieving specific objectives;

establishment of procedures for implementing modifications in programs when needed.

Faculty Involvement in Learning Resources Center Planning

The degree and levels of faculty involvement in learning resources center planning will be instrumental in determining the effectiveness of the center. On the highest level, for instance, the Carnegie Commission (1972, p. 51) recommends:

> Institutions of higher education should contribute to the advancement of instructional technology not only by giving favorable consideration to expanding its use, whenever such use is appropriate, but also to placing responsibility for its introduction and utilization at the highest possible level of academic administration.

Such administrative involvement is a key requirement. However, although we do not recommend that a faculty committee administer the learning resources center, the value of the faculty advisory committees should also be recognized. On the planning level, for developing the philosophy and objectives of the learning resources center, a committee of academic representatives from each school can be most beneficial. The committee would examine the plans of each school for the use of learning resources, arrive at a fair consensus of the actual needs of each school, and reach agreement as to what should be done to support such needs.

Another important communication vehicle is through learning resources liaison representatives from academic and organized research units. These liaison representatives are kept up to date on new developments that may be useful to their organizations—developments which include teaching methods, new media and materials, and other services offered by the learning resources center. They can insure that any pertinent information is routed to the appropriate members of their department. They need only be involved in the significant matters that apply to their own organization and should not be bothered with routine requests for slides, charts, television, and other services. The designation of the liaison representative insures personal contact between the learning resources center and someone in each department competent to speak in the department's best interests.

Ad hoc committees selected from the roster of liaison representatives can be useful for specific inputs and advice. For example, an Ad Hoc Price and Rate Committee set up on an annual basis to review the learning resources center recharge structure and to consider recommended changes has been found to be an excellent means of insuring faculty understanding and acceptance of the learning resources center Price and Rate Schedule on at least one University of California campus.

BUDGETING

Four kinds of budget, from the least to the most desirable, have been identified by Horton and Bishop (1970):

1. The *no budget* budget, closely related to emotional appeals and subjective value judgments, is tied to available funds. Funds are divided from a central office on a first-come, first-serve basis, with each department obtaining its share, generally an augmentation or reduction of the previous years' funding. Additional funds can often be obtained during the year,

until the central office funds are depleted. Decisions regarding funding are not based on programs. Hopefully, this type of budget is disappearing.

2. The *line item* budget is one where the central office receives information from the using department, relative to funding levels for each kind of need, in advance. The items of expenditure are listed and a specific amount of money is allocated to each line item. The central office reviews the line items based on priorities as seen from the top. The department governs its own funding affairs within the limits set up for each line item, such as telephone, travel, office supplies, film, equipment.

3. The *performance budget* is based on functions and/or activities, generally by department, and is concerned with the significance of the services to be performed. Yearly funding allocations are based on individual department priorities and needs to carry out performance functions. Departments are managers of specific fund categories, but are not restricted to line item constraints.

4. The *Planning-Programming-Budgeting System (PPBS)*, considers the entire system, by program, projected one or more years. It examines the relationship between the budget program and objectives of the organization. It seeks the flexible use of budget through the relationship of resources used for specific programs and the products of these programs, not just either set of data alone.

PPBS is the most meaningful and effective budget system. It is recommended by Horton and Bishop (1970), by Brown, Norberg, and Srygley (1972), and by Hartley (1968), among others. The implementation of PPBS or equivalent procedures is essential to the fulfillment of the learning resources center mission in the overall university education and research program.

The Planning-Programming-Budgeting System (PPBS) and the Learning Resources Center

PPBS consists of four steps: planning, programming, budgeting, and evaluation. The same procedure is followed for the total university organization, or for any unit of the university system, including the learning resources center.

In *planning*, operational objectives are determined. As pointed out in Chapter 3, if learning resources are to contribute their full potential to the improvement of teaching, it is not only desirable, but *necessary,* for the learning resources center to be integrally related to the full process of educational planning. However, this is far too seldom the case:

> If media specialists are consulted about curriculum and organization at all, it is usually after key decisions have been made. As a result, schools and colleges usually make little effort to weave new kinds of materials and modes of instruction into the fabric of the institution (Commission on Instructional Technology, 1970, p. 83).

Until this relationship and involvement is clearly defined and accepted by university administrators, the center will continue to have difficulty in defining its own goals and objectives, will struggle for adequate budget, and will have serious problems in justifying its existence. Inclusion of the center in the full process of educational planning will mean that the learning resources center will no longer have the status of a separate service organization, like "Buildings and Grounds," or "Maintenance," nor will it be considered a program in and of itself, as is usually the case.

How can the learning resources center involve itself? A simple and direct way would be the requirement that each university indicate in its Academic Plan or similar plan* how it is using learning resources in its programs. The Academic Plan would be submitted to the University Academic Planning and Program Review Board, which would evaluate the plan from a university-wide perspective. Thus, a Chancellor would review the various programs under his control in the light of learning resources center participation, which would generate communication and involvement with the learning resources center director. This one move could bring deans and administrators into

*Each university or institution may have its own variation of such a plan depending on the number of campuses in the university and the amount of administrative decentralization, Academic Plan here usually means a campus-wide plan.

dialogue with the learning resources center about common goals and objectives immediately. In this way, the university administration will provide the leadership and support that will enable the learning resources center to operate effectively.

On the level of PPBS for the learning resources center, the center staff and representatives of the academic clientele will use the information developed on academic-level planning to determine the operational objectives of the center. They will comprise the planning staff which will identify the needs the learning resources center is to meet and which will inventory existing as well as desired activities of the center. From this they will develop a statement of the learning resources philosophy and objectives, the purpose of the planning stage.

In *programming,* the actual performance programs are designed. Once again, input from the learning resources center staff and the academic clients will be instrumental. Based on the philosophy and objectives developed in the planning stage, staff and academic representatives will develop the overall learning resources center program. The program describes the activities of the learning resources center in terms of resources and program elements. The center program includes the program designs for the individual subunits of the center and the programs designed for the various production or presentation outputs. Detailed statements of programs are essential for implementation within the learning resources center, but it is recommended that a general statement be prepared for the edification of the academic clientele.

In *budgeting,* the necessary resources are allocated to accomplish the specific goals and objectives of the various programs. Budgeting provides the financial data to support the statements of plans and programs. The financial plans are derived from the long-range program plans. It is again recommended that both a detailed document for learning resources center implementation and a public document for the clientele be prepared.

In the budget the planning is resolved, and through the budget programs are realized. The following purposes are served by the budget:

specification of educational and research goals in financial terms;

identification of important components in the management of money, facilities, and personnel;

evaluation of operations;

facilitation of control of expenditures;

an accounting of financial management.

In essence, the budget is the means by which money can be made to work for established objectives.

Evaluation, the final step in PPBS, deals primarily with program evaluation. Based on this evaluation, goals and objectives are revised and modified, new objectives are determined, new programs designed, and priorities reassessed. Considering the learning resources center as an integral part of the education and research system, the most important measure of its performance would be evidence indicating the contribution of learning resources to the learning achievements of the students and the communication of research findings. This aspect of evaluation of the center was discussed in Chapter 3.

At the end of the evaluation process, it is necessary to determine:

how to provide funds for those programs which will continue at their present levels;

how to provide greater support for expanding programs or lessen support for contracting ones so that they can function efficiently and effectively;

how to make funds available for new programs;

what capital outlay programs are required to implement the ongoing, expanded, and new learning resources center programs.

A key quality of program budgeting is its capacity to promote fiscal flexibility. Program budgeting assumes that management has the authority to choose appropriate courses of action, at its own discretion, so long as it achieves program objectives satisfactorily. The program budget is thus not a straitjacket to enforce predetermined courses of action; it is an instrument for identifying levels and kinds of support to be provided to accomplish intended purposes. Additionally, however, use of program budgeting carries with it the responsibility for management to provide evidence (hopefully objective) of having achieved goals as intended (Brown, Norberg, and Srygley, 1972).

With the program budgeting concept, the inviolability of existing programs is more likely to be challenged. Furthermore, an on-going evaluation of outputs and cost of existing programs would be required, and alternative solutions along with comparative costs and anticipated outputs would be expected with new proposals. With this approach, budgetary planning can become one of positive action to achieve long-range goals (Hartley, 1968).

ADMINISTRATION

Planning, coordinating, and controlling are the major functions of management. A successful organization is one in which human and nonhuman resources are organized in an efficient and effective way. Effective coordination is directly related to good organization and has as its purpose the best quality performance at the least expense.

Proper accounting and budgeting will provide management with reliable facts, figures, and interpretations with which the organization can operate more efficiently and economically. Accounting procedures must conform to the plans of management. Accounting records and reports should be designed to reflect costs and performance in relation to clearly defined, specific responsibilities.

Accounting reports made to different levels of management are means to facilitate control. These reports should be concerned with the costs and operations under the control of the manager to whom they are provided. Past perfromance is one good basis for comparison in evaluating current data. Forms and bookkeeping records are also excellent control mechanisms. These documents should be designed to meet the needs of the individual operations they are intended to implement and should be continually evaluated to make certain that they are effective.

Business Management

It is extremely valuable to have a staff member within the learning resources center organization who is responsible for

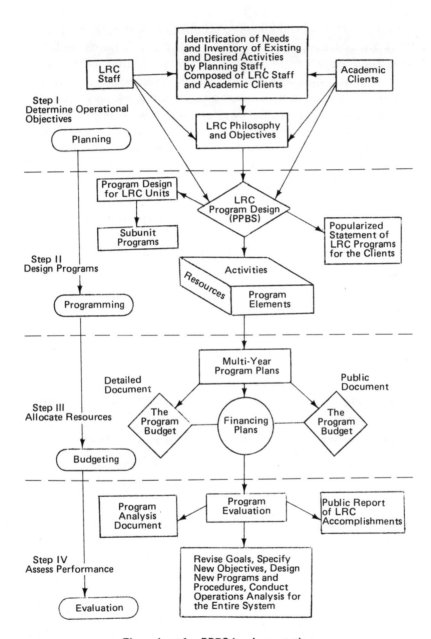

Flow chart for PPBS implementation

After Harry J. Hartley, EDUCATIONAL PLANNING-PROGRAMMING-BUDGETING: A Systems Approach, © 1968, p. 158. Adapted by permission of Prentice-Hall, Inc., Englewood Cliffs, New Jersey.

ensuring that the bookkeeping, accounting, and budgeting functions are not only appropriate for the center's needs, but also that they operate effectively. A learning resources center business manager, not only trained and experienced in accounting and business management, but also with a working knowledge and understanding of the development, use, production, and presentation of learning resources, can be invaluable serving in a staff position to the director. The manager's responsibility should not be limited to accounting and financial matters, but should include reviewing and evaluating all aspects of management control. Such a person should check to see that the learning resources center policies and procedures are being implemented, and evaluate the effectiveness of the policies and procedures in furthering the objectives of the center.

The business manager must be expert in the analysis of data and the preparation of written reports. In a staff position, he advises and recommends, but he has no line responsibility over general operations. In this respect, he can have a comfortable staff relationship to the operational managers as well, advising and consulting with them on an equal basis. Other responsibilities include:

designing and operation of all learning resources center accounting records;

preparing and analyzing financial statements and reports;

preparing and/or coordinating the preparation of cost standards, rate schedules, income forecasts, and capital improvement programs, as well as the budgets;

comparing performance with budget standards, and submiting reports and analyses based on same to the proper managers;

developing and implementing internal controls and audits.

Only the smallest learning resources center can function efficiently without the full-time services of such a specialist. Even in a small learning resources center, the director needs a staff member on whom to rely for handling these functions. In this case, the functions can be included as job responsibilities of the administrative assistant.

Budget Administration

The budget and accounting systems should be designed to facilitate operations as much as possible, but should only be as extensive and expensive as they are worthwhile in providing useful information. Duplication of central accounting records should be avoided, but a system that will provide a double check on these records is advisable.

Every effort must be made to follow the plans and procedures set up to implement the budget, yet the administration should be flexible enough to handle emergencies and unpredictable circumstances. Good management and planning go hand in hand and the director has every right to expect that agreed-upon plans and procedures will be followed.

The staff function of facilitating the budget process should not be confused with the departmental line functions. Line management makes the decisions, the budget staff assists the line organization.

The principal responsibilities of the staff member responsible for the budget (or business manager) are:

to counsel and advise the operational managers in regard to the budget during the budget preparation period;

to supply these managers with data on which to base their budget estimates;

to evaluate each unit budget and make appropriate recommendations;

to evaluate and revise the budget data collected and assemble same in accordance with the overall leraning resources center budget plan;

to submit the complete budget to the director, along with comments, interpretations, and recommendations, so that he has all the facts needed to make final acceptance or rejection decisions;

to issue periodic—monthly, quarterly, annual, or as needed—reports showing achieved results compared with the budget;

to prepare statistical studies and statements as required by management;

to recommend actions designed to improve efficiency where necessary.

The value of the budget process and administration in making and coordinating plans can be seen in the above description. The budget is also useful as a communications device, through the exchange of quantitative information about objectives and limitations. It may also serve as a standard for measuring actual performance, by seeking the answer to the question, "Have we done as we planned to do?" It is a valuable aid to control, since planning and coordination are prerequisites of control and it assists in the integration of objectives among unit managers.

Budget Preparation

The program budget is concerned with the allocation of the resources necessary to accomplish the specific goals and objectives of the various learning resources centers programs. More people than the director and the business manager should be involved in developing the learning resources center budget and preparing the program statement justifications and cost estimates. Ideally, inputs from the learning resources center staff and the academic clientele have already determined the programs which the budget is designed to implement. It would also be beneficial to include as participants as many people as possible affected by the budget decisions.

The budget should be built up by program unit areas and should show the controllable fiscal data for each area of responsibility. Responsible supervisors should participate in the process of setting up budgetary goals and figures, and should agree to their reasonableness. If they are not so involved, they are not likely to have a constructive attitude toward the budget. It is important that these supervisors have a complete understanding of the budget process. This means continual discussions of the actual results achieved in relation to the budgeted anticipations.

It is important, also, to distinguish between the two primary fiscal aspects of management, accounting and budgeting. Accounting is concerned with recording (bookkeeping), reporting, and interpreting financial activities. It is essentially involved with historical, or past events. Budgeting is concerned with planning for the future. A good deal of this planning derives from the historical accounting records, and the value and significance of budgets can be evaluated by comparison with the actual events, as they take place, in the accounting records. Therefore, there should be a similarity in form and meaning between the two, in order to facilitate this comparison. Development of account classifications should take into consideration this dual function.

The budget figures for each area of responsibility should be based on goals that the area can be reasonably expected to achieve. If too much is expected, frustration will surely result. If too little is expected, standards may become relaxed. Budgets should be prepared in sufficient detail to permit adequate analysis and explanation of deviations from expected results, and to facilitate the adjustment of plans to meet changed conditions. Revisions and modifications should be made when conditions have changed materially, indicating that the original figures are unrealistic or in error. When comparing actual performance with the budget, the exceptions, or, data significantly different from those anticipated are of particular importance.

Although it might seem desirable to present a model learning resources center budget, we have been unable to find a simple, easy method for deriving one, and the literature is not helpful in this respect. There are good reasons for this. First, there is a lack of solid operational data from a variety of active learning resources centers on which to base generalizable formulae, cost estimates, planning criteria, and the like. Hopefully, a national study of the data derived from such centers can be programmed in the near future as primary source material. Second, at this time it may be better to suggest general guidelines and procedures than to create a hypothetical learning resources center budget. This is in keeping with the general approach in preceding chapters stressing the uniqueness of each learning resource center situation and the fact that budgets as well as other management devices should be designed for particular situations. There is no "average learning resources center" because the cost of operating is not only a function of student enrollment but of degree of faculty involvement.

Such a budget document is mainly a compilation of program and subprogram descriptions, presented individually with explanatory narrative supported by pertinent detailed data and budget figures. With ongoing programs, historical data are included, as well as program projections beyond the budget year. New programs have justifying data and pertinent projection information. The budget figures are then summarized and organized in keeping with the learning resources center organization structure. Each program exposition has a similarity of structure to facilitate understanding and evaluation. One form the expositions might take follows the format of a grant proposal abstract:

Title of program,
Description of program,
Supporting data and justifications,
Historical perspective information,
Program budget figures.

Adequate and Meaningful Record Keeping

The criterion for the adequacy of record keeping (beyond what is needed in order to transact normal day-to-day functions) is the degree to which meaningful statements and reports can be prepared from the records the center keeps. The purposes of statements and reports are to:

provide administrators with necessary information regarding financial conditions, transactions, and their results;

provide data for decision making;

provide data to administrators for use in policy determinations and in making evaluations;

provide data for developing future plans;

provide a history of financial activities, policies, and trends;

summarize statistics to provide information requested by various interested and involved agencies and individuals.

The records should, at least, provide the following data, preferably by program or type of service, as bases for reports and statements:

operating income by source (direct support, grant, recharge, etc.);

item production showing recharged time, where applicable;

expenditures for salaries, materials, and equipment;

number of presentations;

number of equipment loans;

number of media (films, videotapes, etc.) rentals and book-ings.

Valuable as these data may be in terms of implementing the purposes stated above, information derived from outside the individual center is much to be desired if quantitative evaluation of the performance of the learning resources center is to be realized. The lacking of standardization in record keeping and the development of criteria for operating data relating to learn-ing resources centers in general severely limit the degree to which comparisons can be made.

"At present, cost data on educational technology are almost nonexistent. The lack of these data severely impedes the aca-demic decision making process. Regardless of costing proce-dures used, ways must be found to place costs of educational technology in perspective. Present inadequate cost data are frequently so subjective that they are nothing more than pious hopes. We must come to grips with the reality of cost analysis in the academic decision making process." (Brown, Norberg, and Srygley, 1972, p. 24.)

Until such data are available, vital functions such as setting up budgets for learning resources centers subunits and structur-ing recharges must be based primarily on the historical experi-ence of the individual center.

The following statement is a summary of information receiv-ed from 17 learning resources center directors by the University of Wisconsin-Green Bay Informal Survey of Instructional Re-sources Funding made in 1971:

Almost every instructional resources administrator responding to the survey letter has established a policy of collecting data showing the quality and quantity of services being rendered to students and faculty. However, this effort has not always paid dividends when submitted as justification for funding requests.

A significant number of respondents noted that easily obtained statistics such as student-teacher ratios and enrollment data are virtually worthless in substantiating budget requests.

More successful has been the submission of a combination of statistical background plus written justification explaining the need for each item listed.

Promising approaches discovered through this survey include: (1) justification based on dollars spent per student served; (2) justification relating dollars spent to level of equipment use and services rendered, if these elements can be accurately defined; (3) requiring staff members to keep daily or weekly logs of their activity to determine whether time has in fact been spent in accordance with administrative priorities; and (4) a private survey eliciting budget information from several comparable institutions each year, citing these figures as justification.

SPECIAL BUDGETARY CONSIDERATIONS

Direct Learning Resources Center Budget and the Recharged Budget Supplement

The acceptance of the importance of learning resources as an integral part of academic and research programs also means the provision of sufficient direct budgetary support to allow the center to develop and grow along with these programs. Recognition includes developing a reasonable policy for supplementing the direct budget through recharges, an approach beneficial to all. Policies which anticipate that recharges to client departments can finance increased costs resulting from increased need and utilization while direct support from the university decreases, are not realistic or reasonable in light of the rapidity of growth and the increased importance of learning resources. This growth is more of a revolutionary change than a regular development related to enrollment, and must be treated as such. Developing recharges into the primary budget base may be proper for luxury items (which slides and films admittedly were at one time) but as learning resources become more and more central to the academic processes, they cease to be luxuries.

National surveys, such as the Duke University Medical Center Division of Audiovisual Education Survey of Audiovisual Facilities, in March 1972, show that zero direct support budget learning resources centers are the least successful centers in the country. The centers performing at the most efficient levels are those with the greatest direct support. Primary dependence on recharges encourages maintenance of the status quo. This practice not only limits growth and discourages experimentation and innovation, but may perpetuate inefficient and costly methods. Raising prices may seem like a simple and reasonable solution, but the center will very quickly price itself out of existence if its prices exceed its clients' ability or willingness to pay. The university must support the growth of any campus-wide activity, if it is to remain viable.

Recharges are generally expected to provide some degree of policing and self-regulation. A greater degree of control in the learning resources center is made possible by providing a level of direct budgetary support that will insure that the faculty will come to the center for learning resources and not pursue the more costly expedient of producing the resources within their own departments or by using outside producers. The minimum direct support needed to maintain a viable learning resources center should provide for equipment replacement, research and development, instructional development, group and self-instructional presentation services, and planning services. Recharges can only be expected to pay a portion of the production services cost.

The question is not direct budget support vs. recharges, but how much of each? That is not to say that a combination of direct support and supplemental recharge is always an ideal situation, but the current budget climate throughout the academic world leaves little choice. There are advantages in having some recharges. They allow for expansion and contraction of staff and services within a budget year, when needed. They provide a way to order priorities in handling production workloads, by adding special charges for rush work. Recharges also provide a means of utilizing Federal and other grant funds, through charges against research activities, and help reduce the production of unnecessary resources by applying some of the cost of production against the budget of the actual user.

Recharges, however, cannot be expected to support classroom or self-instructional facilities. At best, they can only provide the materials used in these facilities.

Percentage of support should vary according to the type of service involved. Comparing notes with learning resources center directors nationwide shows that Educational Television services require virtually 100 per cent support, Graphics Production services 50 to 60 per cent, and Photography Services 20 to 25 per cent. These percentages are based on what the user can realistically be expected to pay for these services on a recharge basis and still maintain a viable, competitive center.

EQUIPMENT REPLACEMENT

The importance of providing for the orderly replacement of learning resources equipment before it wears out or becomes obsolete must not be underestimated. An instructional program can be seriously affected by equipment failure during a class session, especially when the equipment is essential to the presentation of instructional materials.

A good program for equipment replacement would insure that up-to-date equipment, in good working order, is available for use when most advantageous educationally. Instruction is not at its best when it has to be rearranged to suit equipment availability. The replacement program should therefore include all classroom and self-instruction audiovisual equipment, as well as television hardware and photographic and graphic equipment. The program must take into account the expected useful life of a piece of equipment and insure replacement before the equipment would either be expected to perform below average efficiency or be too costly to maintain. Average equipment "down" time would also be a factor in determining the amount of equipment needed and the expected life of same.

In anticipation of an overall learning resources equipment average life of less than 10 years, a minimum of 10 per cent of inventory value should be set aside annually for replacements (Brown, Norberg, and Srygley, 1972, p. 369). A $500,000 inventory would, therefore, require $50,000 a year for replacements alone, in addition to the funds needed for new equipment to meet increased or different needs and for the repair and maintenance of old equipment. Each piece of equipment should be assigned a replacement date, one which the best information available determines to be somewhat ahead of the expected threshhold of marginal performance.

It has been suggested that periodic minor capital improvement grants can be used for equipment replacement. This procedure might be expeditious where such grants are easier to realize than increases in budget support. Unfortunately, equipment is not so structured that large groups break down or need replacement at given periodic intervals, especially when the equipment is not purchased in large lots. It is much more likely that some will fail each year. An annual replacement program will be the most economical in the long run, and may also provide a surplus of functioning, replaced items, which may not be usable in routine situations, but can still be serviceable for emergency use or in times when demands exceed normal supplies.

Research and Development

Academic department budgets are not geared to the research and development of learning resources. In fact, departments can sometimes barely afford the routine learning resources center services, let alone developmental funds. Therefore, it is unrealistic to expect that interdepartmental recharges can provide the supplementary budget needed for this function. For example, given routine annual budgeting procedures, the high initial cost of the instructional development of self-instructional materials puts them out of reach, since no academic department could fund this item by recharges from its typical annual budget. Clearly, depending on recharges as the source of budgets for the research and development of learning resources militates against innovation and experimentation.

A change in instructional program requiring learning resources development is also better handled by the center than by a faculty pilot program, because the center can draw on its resources and expertise. Introducing a substantial innovation such as an Instructional Development Unit is a learning resources center function. First, enough money is necessary for it to be set up by the center and used by the faculty for a reasonable period of time. Then, faculty and administration representatives can confer with the director, make the necessary evaluation, and decide if the innovation is to continue. Support for a learning resources center pilot program encourages widespread experimental use and insures that the project gets a fair trial.

The learning resources field is in a state of flux and rapid development. The center that lacks research and development funds to innovate and experiment will atrophy if academic departments are forced to pursue expedient (and often more expensive) means of developing new methods by themselves. Providing research and development funds for the learning resources center may be the most crucial policy decision affecting the future of the center, because without such funds the center cannot move beyond the status quo.

The experience gained from research and development activities on the part of the learning resources center should be available to all, not merely to a single department or school. Research and development is as important to a successful learning resources center as research is to an academic department in its field.

There are opportunities for innovation and improvement funds through grants and capital outlay programs. These opportunities cannot be fully realized unless provisions are also made for operating funds beyond the grant period. It is therefore very important that faculty and administration are committed to an evaluation procedure that is binding upon them, in terms of continuing support, at the time that the pilot project is proposed.

High Initial Cost of Technology

The Carnegie Commission report, *The Fourth Revolution* (1972, p. 3), states that "for financing authorities, the new informational technology will eventually reduce instructional costs below levels possible using conventional methods alone, but, in the short run, it will only increase costs." Budgeting in public universities is normally locked into a one-year cycle and with no provision for accumulating funds over a period of years nor for prepayment of future budgeting funds. Under such conditions, it is virtually impossible to build into a learning resources center budget the money necessary to implement a technological revolution, especially considering the high cost of equipment. The funds required to get over this "initial hump" must be therefore included in planning the learning resource center programs, with the recognition that, as the use of learning resources increases, the cost of learning resources in relation to the total Instruction and Research (I & R) Budget will probably decrease. At the University of California, for example, current use of learning resources is funded by a much smaller percentage of I & R budgets than the percentage of student time involving learning resources to total student learning time (1.5 vs. 5 per cent; see footnote on p. 83). Full realization of the recommended criterion of 10 per cent of student time can be effected by substantially less than twice the current learning resources center budgets.

"We are confident that the expanding instructional technology will improve learning, make learning and teaching more challenging to students and teachers alike, and yield cost savings as it becomes more widely used and reduces the need for live instruction. It may, indeed, provide the best means available to us for solving the difficult problem of continuing to educate growing numbers of students of all ages within a budget the American people can afford." (Carnegie Commission, 1972, p. 86.)

Developing New Learning Resource Centers

Both the development of a new learning resources center where no learning resources facilities of a centralized nature exist, and the housing of facilities in operation at various locations in a central, unified center, are of concern to fiscal planners. Although it may no longer be necessary to justify the need for learning resources, it may still be difficult to justify the centralized facility, since it may threaten the continuance of departmental facilities and give the impression that a new, sophisticated center may be underutilized. Proper long-range planning will start the center off reasonably equipped for current needs, and allow the learning resources center to develop along with the programs it is intended to serve. The center needs time to develop experience regarding faculty use and the potentials for interdepartmental recharging, so that a viable center can function and grow. Such a procedure was used at the University of Connecticut's Biomedical Communications Center (BMC). According to the BMC Annual Report for 1970-71,

"Having developed the price list, a 'dry run' fiscal year (April, 1970, to April, 1971) was undertaken to test its validity . . . . Costs were compared to the ersatz income on a monthly basis, and records were kept as if billing was actually being processed."

This procedure demonstrates a most desirable sensitivity. Often a new center is given a recharge commitment difficult for an established center to support. Faculty members are reluctant to patronize a new facility with which they have had no experience, especially when there is no record of performance on which to justify prices. A new center requires substantial subsidy to get under way, and a program of experimentation and evaluation, especially when implementing a recharge structure.

SUMMARY

A budget is a financial expression of the objectives, programs, and activities of an organization. Proper planning and coordinated activity precede and determine the budget statement. The budget should be a narrative plan of operations supported by figures, not figures supported by narrative explanation.

The Planning-Programming-Budgeting System (PPBS) can help in choosing and implementing programs, and in organizing and utilizing personnel, materials, and facilities to realize identifiable goals, within the framework of available funds. Proper accounting and budgeting, coordinated by a business manager for the learning resources center, can provide the director with reliable facts, figures, and interpretations to operate the center more efficiently and economically.

Budget preparation results from careful examination of all operational aspects of the learning resources center. The budget coordinates the activities of all parts of the organization and permits frequent comparison of actual events with expectations, so that modifications can be made as needed. Good management uses the budget as a tool for effecting change and improvement, recognizing that learning resources support teaching and research, and are not ends in themselves. The budget is the means by which money can be made to work for quality.

The learning resources center budget should be planned as a tool for the systematic accomplishment of the educational and research program goals. The long-term budget is a plan for change that aims to eliminate crises and emergencies. At the very least, it should be effective in minimizing them. It can only be effective to the degree that it can anticipate teaching and research needs and the resources necessary to meet them. Therefore, it is based on effective forecasting of future programs.

Short-term budgets are most effective when they relate to the long-term budget. They must conform to the long-range goals if they are to be meaningful, and should be concerned not only with implementing and developing the long-range plans but with making them fit current conditions. Phasing in and out of programs should be done in an orderly way, with the least strain on finances and personnel. Constant evaluation and modification are necessary if the plans are to remain viable.

Recharges to client departments cannot be expected to provide the major support for a learning resources center. A level of support must be provided through general university fund sources that will insure that the center does not price itself out of existence. The minimum subsidy support that can maintain a viable center must provide for equipment replacement, research and development, instructional development, group and self-instructional presentation services, and planning services. Recharges can only be expected to pay toward the cost of production services.

"The modern approach to the planning and budgeting of educational media programs is increasingly influenced by the systems approach and the related concept of program budgeting. Departmental budgets for educational media services should be developed under the leadership of those who administer them, in proper accord with the total instructional program." (Brown, Norberg and Srygley, 1972, p. 381.)

Summary of Criteria and Recommendations

Five criteria are essential in planning a learning resources center for a university campus. Also presented below are three recommendations that probably will become criteria after data resulting from further experience are available. Finally, criteria are seriously needed in two areas. These are presented below with a short explanatory comment and a reference to further information within this book.

CRITERIA

1. **The director of learning resources should report to the chief academic (level-two) officer of the campus.** To report directly to the chief campus administrative (level-one) officer places the director in a position too high to coordinate well with other leaders of the campus educational program. To report to a level-three administrative officer or the dean of a particular school also prevents him from coordinating well and indicates to the campus that the activity may be regarded as a low-level, low-priority service function. (See pp. 37-38.)

2. **The director of learning resources should be a professional member of the faculty, having qualified according to high standards of academic preparation as well as experience.** With

an orientation toward the improvement of college teaching, competence in curriculum improvement, and skill in working with faculty who are interested in improving their teaching, the director merits their respect and acceptance. Without these qualifications, he is no more than a distributor of materials and repairer of equipment. (See pp. 34-35.)

3. **At least one consultant in instructional development should be employed full time on the learning resources center staff.** This area is described as having the greatest potential for the improvement of instruction during the coming decade. As the instructor moves away from mere *informing* toward a more truly professional role of *teaching* a consultant in instructional development becomes an important resource to the campus educational program. The consultant's skills are valuable in insuring that production and presentation services, if used, are used with maximum effectiveness. This expertise is also required in support of educational planning services provided by the learning resources center to academic department chairmen and deans. (See pp. 22-25 and 31-33.)

4. **The number of staff and square feet of space for the learning resources center should be determined by type and scope of service, enrollment, and percentage of learning time as shown in Tables 4-12.** No single staff-to-space ratio can be applied to all learning resources center buildings on general campuses, because there is no standard or typical center size that is appropriate to all campuses. Each center is thus designed to support the particular instructional program of a given campus. The staff and space criteria in these tables allow maximum flexibility to campus planners. (See Chapter 4.)

5. **The budget of the learning resources center should be determined according to the Planning-Programming-Budgeting System or an equivalent procedure.** The learning resources center tends to be seen only as a program in and of itself unless its contribution is tied to the campus educational program through planning. Unlike the one-year budget cycle, PPBS or an equivalent procedure provides evaluative and control mechanisms appropriate to programming long range economies and improvement of teaching despite higher initial costs. (See Chapter 5.)

RECOMMENDATIONS

1. **The learning resources center should offer training in the application of improved instructional strategies to faculty members on a continuing basis.** Too many outstanding courses that make use of innovative techniques deteriorate because the replacement teacher has not been trained in their use. (See pp. 45-46.)

2. **Space for the learning resources center should be sufficiently convenient and attractive to encourage faculty acceptance and utilization.** "New media" services that are housed in the basements of the oldest buildings on campus have not in general proved highly successful. (See pp. 81-82.)

3. **Direct funding for the learning resources center should be available in an amount necessary to provide for equipment replacement, research and development, consultation in instructional development, group and self-instructional presentation services, and planning services as a minimum; the balance should be obtained on a fee-for-service (recharge) basis.** Centers with little or no direct support are the least successful in the country. (See pp. 100-102.)

AREAS SERIOUSLY NEEDING CRITERIA

1. **Development of a criterion for the effective delivery of educational planning services is a crucial current need.** Vigorous efforts to solve the substantive and procedural aspects of this problem may well result in the elimination of obstacles that prevent optimum use of available learning resources. (See pp. 33.)

2. **Development of a criterion for administrative and geographical decentralization is currently needed.** A reasonable policy must be developed to avoid the undesirable extremes of overcentralization and fragmentation. (See pp. 40-44.)

References

Allen, A.R. "Survey of Positions and Salaries of the Biomedical Communications Staff." Paper presented at the Conference of Directors of Biomedical Communication. Atlanta: October 1971.

American Library Association (Association of College and Research Libraries), American Association of Community and Junior Colleges, Association for Educational Communications and Technology. "Guidelines for Two-Year College Learning Resources Programs." *Audiovisual Instruction,* Vol. 18, January 1973, pp. 50–61.

American Library Association and National Education Association. *Standards for School Media Programs.* Chicago: ALA, 1969.

Association for Educational Communications and Technology and American Library Association. *Media Programs: District and School.* Washington and Chicago: AECT and ALA, 1972.

Audio-Visual Aids in Higher Scientific Education. Report of the Brynmor Jones Committee. Great Britain: H.M. Stationery Office, 1965.

Baker, R. L. and Schutz, R.E. *Instructional Product Development.* New York: Van Nostrand–Reinhold, 1972.

Barnes O.D. and Schrieber, D. *Computer-Assisted Instruction: A Selected Bibliography.* Washington: Association for Educational Communications and Technology, 1972.

Blancheri, R.L. and Merrill, I.R. "Television in Health Sciences Education: II. The Step Presentation of Dental Technic Instruction." *Journal of Dental Education,* Vol. 27, 1963, pp. 167–170.

Bretz, R. *Communication Media: Properties and Uses.* Memorandum RM 6070-NLM/PR. Santa Monica: RAND Corp., 1969.

Brown, J.W. and Norberg, K.D. *Administering Educational Media.* New York: McGraw-Hill, 1965.

Brown, J.W., Norberg, K.D. and Srygley, S.K. *Administering Educational Media.* New York: McGraw-Hill, 1972.

Campeau, P.L. "Selective Review of the Results of Research on the Use of Audiovisual Media to Teach Adults." *AV Communication Review,* Vol. 22, No. 1, Spring 1974, pp. 5-40.

Carnegie Commission on Higher Education. *The Fourth Revolution: Instructional Technology in Higher Education.* New York: McGraw-Hill, 1972.

Carpenter, M.B. and Haggart, S.A. *Cost Effectiveness Analysis for Educational Planning.* RAND Corp., P4327, March 1970.

Cheit, E.F. *The New Depression in Higher Education.* General Report for the Carnegie Commission on Higher Education and the Ford Foundation. New York: McGraw Hill, 1971.

Chu, G.C. and Schramm, W. *Learning from Television: What the Research Says.* Washington: National Association of Educational Broadcasters, 1967.

Commission on Instructional Technology. *To Improve Learning.* A Report to the President and the Congress of the United States. Washington: U.S. Government Printing Office, March 1970.

Conklin, J.L. "A Two-Year Study of a Self-Instructional Slide-Tape Program." Paper presented at the Ninth Annual Conference on Research in Medical Education. Association of American Medical Colleges. Los Angeles: October 1970.

Curl, D.H. "The Self-Instructional Audio-Visual Laboratory." *Educational Screen and Audio-Visual Guide,* Vol. 46, May 1967, pp. 24—25.

deGroot, J., "How Self-Instruction Works in a Basic Science." Paper presented at the Seminar on Effective Use of Self-Instruction in the Health Sciences. San Francisco: University of California, October 1970.

Department of Audiovisual Instruction. *Quantitative Standards for Audiovisual Personnel, Equipment and Materials in Elementary, Secondary and Higher Education.* Washington: DAVI, 1966. (mimeo).

Dubin, R. and Taveggia, T.C. *The Teaching-Learning Paradox: A Comparative Analysis of College Teaching.* Eugene, Ore: Center for the Advanced Study of Educational Administration, University of Oregon, 1968, Monograph No. 18, p. 13.

Duke University. *Survey of Audiovisual Facilities.* Chapel Hill, N.C.: Duke University Medical Center, Division of Audiovisual Education, March 1972.

Erickson, C.W.H. *Administering Instructional Media Programs.* New York: Macmillan, 1968.

Fagan, B.M. "Learning Archaeology: The Use of Multi-Media in a Lower Division Course." *Experiment and Innovation,* Vol. 4, May 1971, p. 40.

Gage, N.L. "Paradigms for Research on Teaching." In Gage, N.L. (Ed.), *Handbook of Research on Teaching.* Chicago: Rand McNally, 1963.

Gagne, R.M. "Learning Theory, Educational Media, and Individualized Instruction," *Educational Broadcasting Review,* Vol. 4, June 1970, pp. 49—62.

Glaser, R. (Ed.). *Teaching Machines and Programmed Learning: II. Data and Directions.* Washington: Association for Educational Communications and Technology, 1965.

Hamlin, O. and Sprinkle, M.D. "New Concepts of Media and their Management at the University of Kentucky Medical Center."*Drexel Library Quarterly,* Vol. 7, April 1971, pp. 137—144.

Hartley, H.J. *Educational Planning-Programing-Budgeting.* Englewood Cliffs: Prentice-Hall, 1968.

Hitch, C.J. "Instructions to Appointment and Promotion Committees." *University Bulletin, a Weekly Bulletin for the Staff of the University of California,* Vol. 18, 1969, pp. 30—32.

Hoban, C.F. and van Ormer, E.B. *Instructional Film Research 1918—1950 (Rapid Mass Learning).* Technical Report No. SDC 269-7-19, Contract N60 Onr-269, T.O. VII, Departments of the Army and the Navy with Pennsylvania State College. Port Washington, L.I., N.Y.: Special Devices Center, U.S. Navy, 1951.

116   REFERENCES

Hooper, R. "A Diagnosis of Failure." *AV Communication Review,* Vol. 17, No. 3, Fall 1969, pp. 245–264.

Horton, R.I. and Bishop, K.W. "Keeping Up With the Budget Crunch." *Audiovisual Instruction,* Vol. 15, December 1970, p. 49.

Hubiak, G. "Condensed Curricula." *Synapse,* Vol. 15, November 6, 1970, p. 3.

Kinder, J.S. *Audio-Visual Materials and Techniques.* New York: American Book, 1950.

Larson, L.C. *Instructional Technology Graduate Degree Programs in U.S. Colleges and Universities, 1969–71.* Washington: Association for Educational Communications and Technology, 1971.

"Learning Resources Center." *Planning Guide for Project 908074.* Santa Barbara: University of California, July 1969, p. 8.

Lee, A.M. "Instructional Systems: Which One?" *Audiovisual Instruction,* Vol. 15, January 1970, pp. 30–31

Lumsdaine, A.A., "Instruments and Media of Instruction." *Handbook of Research on Teaching.* In Gage, N.L. (Ed.). Chicago: Rand-McNally, 1963.

McKeachie, W.J. "Research on Teaching at the College and University Level." *Handbook of Research on Teaching.* In Gage, N.L. (Ed.). Chicago: Rand-McNally, 1963.

Merrill, I.R. "Self-instruction within the Medical School Curriculum." Paper presented at the Ninth Annual Conference on Research in Medical Education. Association of American Medical Colleges. Los Angeles, October 1970.

Miller, P.D. "The Relation of Teacher Perceptions of a School's Audio-visual Climate to the Organizational Structure of its Media Program." Paper presented at the Association for Educational Communications and Technology, Detroit, April 1970.

Newman, F. *et al. Report on Higher Education.* Washington: U.S. Government Printing Office, March 1971.

Peterson, G.T. "Graduates of Media Programs in 1972—73." *Audiovisual Instruction,* Vol. 9, March 1974, pp. 26—28.

Peterson, G.T. "Graduates of Media Programs in 1973—74." *Audiovisual Instruction,* Vol. 20, April 1975, pp. 46—49.

Peterson, G.T. "Job Picture Brighter for Graduates of Media Programs in 1974—75." *Audiovisual Instruction*, Vol. 21, April 1976, pp. 9—11.

Ramey, J.W. "The Human Element: Why Non-Print Managers Turn Gray." *Drexel Library Quarterly,* Vol. 7, April 1971, pp. 91—106.

Reid, J.C. and MacLennan, D.W. *Research in Instructional Television and Film.* Washington: U.S. Office of Education, 1967.

Sanford, N. *Where Colleges Fail.* San Francisco: Jossey-Bass, 1968.

Stowe, R. "The Division of Instructional Development." *Audiovisual Instruction,* Vol. 16, June-July 1971, p. 36.

Thornton, J.W. and Brown, J.W. *New Media and College Teaching.* Washington : Association for Educational Communications and Technology, 1968.

University Bulletin, a Weekly Bulletin for the Staff of the University of California. Vol. 19, 1970, p. 71.

University of Connecticut. *Annual Report 1970—71.* Farmington: University of Connecticut, Biomedical Communications Center, September 1971.

University of Wisconsin-Green Bay. *Informal Survey of Instructional Resources Funding.* Green Bay: University of Wisconsin, 1971.

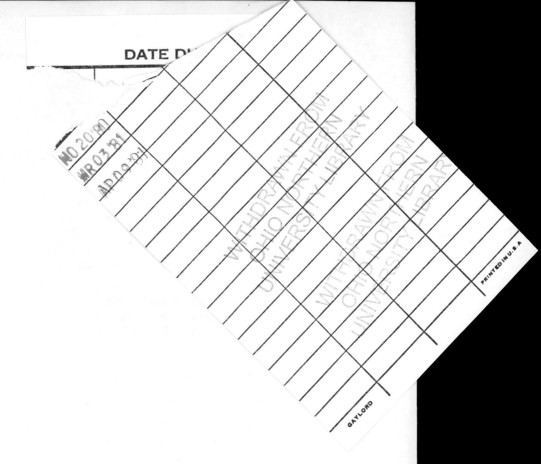